Lindsey Vonn

by Marty Gitlin

LUCENT BOOKS

A part of Gale, Cengage Learning

GALE
CENGAGE Learning·

Detroit • New York • San Francisco • New Haven, Conn • Waterville, Maine • London

B
VonnL
g

LIBRARY OF CONGRESS CATALOGING-IN-PUBLICATION DATA

Gitlin, Marty.
    Lindsey Vonn / Marty Gitlin.
       p. cm. -- (People in the news)
    Summary: "This series profiles the lives and careers of some of today's most
    prominent newsmakers. Whether covering contributions and achievements or
    notorious deeds, books in this series examine why these well-known personages
    garnered public attention"-- Provided by publisher.
    Includes bibliographical references and index.
    ISBN 978-1-4205-0614-3 (hardback)
   1. Vonn, Lindsey--Juvenile literature. 2. Skiers--United States--Biography--Juvenile
literature. I. Title.
    GV854.2.V66G57 2012
    796.93'5092--dc23
    [B]
                                                                        2011047270

Lucent Books
27500 Drake Rd
Farmington Hills MI 48331

ISBN-13: 978-1-4205-0614-3
ISBN-10: 1-4205-0614-5

Printed in the United States of America
1 2 3 4 5 6 7 16 15 14 13 12

10/13

33.95

Contents

Fame and celebrity are alluring. People are drawn to those who walk in fame's spotlight, whether they are known for great accomplishments or for notorious deeds. The lives of the famous pique public interest and attract attention, perhaps because their experiences seem in some ways so different from, yet in other ways so similar to, our own.

Newspapers, magazines, and television regularly capitalize on this fascination with celebrity by running profiles of famous people. For example, television programs such as *Entertainment Tonight* devote all their programming to stories about entertainment and entertainers. Magazines such as *People* fill their pages with stories of the private lives of famous people. Even newspapers, newsmagazines, and television news frequently delve into the lives of well-known personalities. Despite the number of articles and programs, few provide more than a superficial glimpse at their subjects.

Lucent's People in the News series offers young readers a deeper look into the lives of today's newsmakers, the influences that have shaped them, and the impact they have had in their fields of endeavor and on other people's lives. The subjects of the series hail from many disciplines and walks of life. They include authors, musicians, athletes, political leaders, entertainers, entrepreneurs, and others who have made a mark on modern life and who, in many cases, will continue to do so for years to come.

These biographies are more than factual chronicles. Each book emphasizes the contributions, accomplishments, or deeds that have brought fame or notoriety to the individual and shows how that person has influenced modern life. Authors portray their subjects in a realistic, unsentimental light. For example, Bill Gates—the cofounder and former chief executive officer of the software giant Microsoft—has been instrumental in making personal computers the most vital tool of the modern age. Few dispute his business savvy, his perseverance, or his technical expertise, yet critics say he is ruthless in his dealings with competitors and driven more by his desire to maintain Microsoft's dominance in the computer industry than by an interest in furthering technology.

In these books, young readers will encounter inspiring stories about real people who achieved success despite enormous obstacles. Oprah Winfrey—one of the most powerful, most watched, and wealthiest women in television history—spent the first six years of her life in the care of her grandparents while her unwed mother sought work and a better life elsewhere. Her adolescence was colored by pregnancy at age fourteen, rape, and sexual abuse.

Each author documents and supports his or her work with an array of primary and secondary source quotations taken from diaries, letters, speeches, and interviews. All quotes are footnoted to show readers exactly how and where biographers derive their information and provide guidance for further research. The quotations enliven the text by giving readers eyewitness views of the life and accomplishments of each person covered in the People in the News series.

In addition, each book in the series includes photographs, annotated bibliographies, timelines, and comprehensive indexes. For both the casual reader and the student researcher, the People in the News series offers insight into the lives of today's newsmakers—people who shape the way we live, work, and play in the modern age.

Lindsey Vonn: An American Phenomenon

Lindsey Vonn is the most accomplished skier in American history. She won three consecutive World Cup championships, a remarkable feat for a skier—and especially an American, considering the lack of attention paid to the sport in the United States. She also gained rare attention for a skier in her native country by earning an Olympic gold medal in 2010.

Vonn did not reach such lofty heights because of talent alone. She achieved greatness through her mental approach to her performances, understanding the importance of training, and overcoming obstacles in her personal life.

Childhood on the Slopes

Vonn was greatly affected by her upbringing. She lost many of the simple joys of childhood and adolescence to the rigors of training and skiing. She was unable to make many friends in her hometown of Burnsville, Minnesota, because she spent most of her time on the slopes. Her father, former competitive skier Alan Kildow, placed her on a pair of skis at the age of two and encouraged her, sometimes aggressively, throughout her early career.

She was not the only one to sacrifice for her career. Her parents uprooted the family to the skiing hotbed of Vail, Colorado, so she could strengthen her skills and compete more. She felt badly about her siblings having to relocate and wondered if the move played a role in causing the eventual divorce of her parents. Yet she never regretted that her father had introduced her to skiing. She embraced the sport from the beginning and dreamed at an early age of winning multiple Olympic medals. Her determination to be the best skier in the world was instrumental to the success she would eventually enjoy as an adult.

Overcoming Obstacles

Vonn has not had an easy road to greatness. Two critical hurdles—one emotional and one physical—have tested her at recurring times in her career. A key emotional challenge she has faced involves her stormy relationship with her father, who strongly objected to his daughter's romance with her future husband, Thomas Vonn (who is nine years older than her). As she grew closer to Vonn, a former Olympic skier, she grew more distant

Vonn races in a training session in France in 2009. She has achieved great success despite significant physical and personal challenges throughout her career.

from her father. Eventually, she chose to eliminate her dad from her life, a decision that has been emotionally trying at various points during her career.

Lindsey Vonn has also had to overcome many physical injuries sustained via a notoriously brash—or what some critics have called reckless—style on the slopes. Her need for speed in competition causes her to crash often and at quite inopportune times, including during training runs before the 2006 and 2010 Olympics. With help from her husband, Vonn has tempered her aggressive, go-for-broke style a bit, but the desire for speed is not only a part of her personality and skiing strategy, it is also her favorite part of the entire sport. In fact, when a reporter from *Women's Health* asked what her favorite thing about skiing is, she replied, "Being able to go fast! I love the downhill events where we are clocking upwards of 80 miles per hour. Whether it's in my car or when I'm biking or on skis, I just like to push it!"[1]

Vonn's success has resulted in part from her willingness to go faster than other skiers and in part from her ability to stay strong in the face of the obstacles she has faced. As NBC skiing analyst Alan Abrahamson put it when he predicted she would contend for medals in all disciplines at the 2010 Winter Games, "It's not because Lindsey is a proven winner. It's that she's a proven winner because she is so mentally tough."[2]

Maturing to Stardom and Womanhood

Vonn also became a proven winner by dedicating herself to fitness and training. She placed her trust in her husband, who, as a onetime Olympic skier, not only helped her realize the importance of getting in better shape, but also hooked her up with professionals who could design a training regimen specifically for her. That, in turn, gave her strength on the slopes and the consistency required to win medals and championships. If not for her intense desire to blossom into the finest skier in the world, she might not have embraced such a grueling fitness program. Vonn eventually became known for her intense workouts.

Vonn smiles after competing at a World Cup event in Aspen, Colorado, in November 2008. Her success and popularity have made her an ambassador for her sport in the United States.

Although in the United States skiing will likely never be as popular as baseball, football, or basketball, Vonn's triumph in the 2010 Games made her somewhat of a national ambassador for the sport. It generated interest in skiing and transformed her into a star in the United States. She has scaled heights only European athletes had previously reached. And she achieved it with nary a hint of the self-promotion that has plagued many other premier American athletes and alienated fans. In the process she helped place American skiing on the map. She reached the highest echelon of competitive skiing by winning three consecutive World Cup titles.

She is also still motivated. The 2014 Winter Olympics in Sorchi, Russia, await. Whatever she achieves there, one can take heart in the knowledge that Lindsey Vonn will remain the same goal-oriented, unpretentious person she has always been.

Chapter 1

From Turtle to Hare

Linda Krohn was unaware she had a new daughter when she gave birth to Lindsey Kildow on October 18, 1984. The young mother almost did not survive the experience.

Her pregnancy was going well until she awoke that morning with an excruciating headache. She was quickly rushed to the hospital for the delivery. Krohn suffered a stroke during the birth that resulted in minor paralysis in her left leg. She was in a coma for ten days and recalls nothing about the next seven weeks. "Seventy-five percent of the people die from the stroke I had," said Krohn, a successful lawyer. "After five days in the hospital, the nurse came by and said, 'I'm sorry, but your baby needs to leave.' I didn't even understand I had a baby."[3]

Krohn returned to her home in the Minneapolis, Minnesota, suburb of Burnsville for Thanksgiving. She could not remember the name she and husband Alan Kildow had given their daughter. She would have appreciated holding her baby, but she could not. She remained too unsteady on her feet for several months even to cuddle Lindsey in her arms. Krohn eventually recovered enough to provide her daughter with two brothers and two sisters—three of the siblings are triplets.

Chip off the Old Block

Lindsey was born into an athletic family. Her mother had been a fine recreational athlete during her youth. Her father was even more accomplished. He earned three U.S. junior national skiing championships, but his career ended at age eighteen after

A skier glides down a slope at Black Hill Ski Area in Burnsville, Minnesota, where Vonn skied as a young girl.

he suffered a left knee injury while trying out for the Austrian national team. He passed his love of skiing on to his daughter, however, and Kildow had Lindsey on skis by the age of two.

The ambitious toddler slowly navigated tiny hills near her home. A year later she was skiing small slopes at the Buck Hill Ski Area in Burnsville. She would spend so much time there over the next decade that she would later state that Buck Hill and her childhood memories were one and the same. "What I remember most about Buck Hill," she said, "is hot chocolate and sprinkled doughnuts. And Erich."[4]

Erich Sailer was Lindsey's skiing instructor. The first time Alan Kildow brought his six-year-old daughter to him at Buck Hill, Sailer was not impressed. "Poor Alan," Sailer remembers thinking. "He has a real turtle here. She moved extremely slow. She moved like a turtle. So how could I possibly imagine she would be a downhiller?"[5]

Such skepticism would not last. Kildow continued to accompany his daughter to the Buck Hill slopes, and she continued to improve. Buck Hill was not demanding, at least in comparison to more prominent ski areas. It was very small, with a 300-foot (91.44m) slope. Sailer, however, is not only considered one of the finest coaches in Minnesota, but also among the best in the country. He set out to mold Lindsey into one of the premier young skiers in the United States.

Lindsey did not need much pushing at that age. She quickly forged a passion for the sport and a determined will to maximize her potential. Her work ethic helped her improve dramatically. By the age of seven, Lindsey was training by skiing on glaciers in Oregon. Herb Kildow, her grandfather on her father's side, reports that when she was just eight years old, she wrote, "I want to win more medals than anyone ever did"[6] in a school assignment.

Herb Kildow, who had been an avid skier in his younger days, was impressed with the rapid progress made by the young skier. He remembers a conversation he had with his son. "This Lindsey is really going to be something," Herb said to Alan. "Think she'll ever make the Olympics?" Although Alan did not respond, Herb saw a man with a vision. "He was pushing [Lindsey], even when she was young," he said. "He was a man who pushed. He was quite demanding of everybody."[7]

A Mother Misses Out

Whereas her father was demanding, Lindsey's mother was supportive, although from afar. Fallout from the stroke she had suffered at Lindsey's birth made her unable to participate in Lindsey's early life as fully as she would have liked.

The paralysis in her left leg prevented Krohn from traveling to skiing events in which Lindsey competed as a child. That was very frustrating for Krohn, not only because she yearned to watch Lindsey perform. It was also difficult because she too had been an athlete. Krohn could no longer partake in physical activities she enjoyed, much less do them with her daughter.

Krohn's injury made her miss out on a lot of Lindsey's early development as a skier. The paralysis in her leg made it difficult for her to get high enough up the mountain to watch Lindsey

Skiing with Sailer

The 300-foot (91.44 m) slope marking the Buck Hill Ski Area in Minnesota has been described as a "speed bump" compared to the majestic mountains skiers swoosh down in other areas of the world. But Buck Hill coach Erich Sailer has not taken a back-seat to others in grooming pre-mier racers. He

Erich Sailer stands the bottom of a slope at Black Hill Ski Area in Burnsville, Minnesota, where he served as Vonn's first ski coach.

has trained more than twenty-five thousand skiers in more than fifty years of coaching. Many have competed in the World Cup, as well as the Winter Olympics.

Sailer was born and raised in the skiing mecca of Tyrol, Austria. He competed with the Austrian National Class team from 1948 to 1952 before forging a career as an instructor in the United States. He has produced several American Olympians, including gold medalists Lindsey Vonn and Julia Mancuso. In 2005 he was inducted into the U.S. National Ski Hall of Fame.

Austrians are arguably the most passionate skiers and fans of skiing in the world. Sailer has attempted to foster enthusiasm for skiing in America, but he understands it is a tough sell in a country with a wide variety of popular sports. "[Americans] want to know more about skiing, but it is not like the Tyrol where people live and die for skiing," he said.

Austrian Information. "Erich Sailer's Contribution to Ski Coaching in the U.S." December 26, 2007. www.austrianinformation.org/november-december-2007/erich-sailers-contribution-to-ski-coaching-in-the-us.html.

compete in local events. When the girl's growing talent took her to competitions beyond Burnsville, it was even harder for Krohn to keep up. She traveled to Europe with Sailer at the tender age of nine to train without her parents. She continued to win youth events, including a North American junior championship. But Krohn's leg simply would not enable her to scale mountains to watch her daughter display her burgeoning skills.

Lindsey admired her mother because she never heard Krohn complain about the paralysis in her leg, even though Lindsey knew how much she suffered every day. Lindsey's awareness of her mother's trial proved to be inspirational during difficult moments in her own life. "I've never once heard my mom complain about her stroke," Lindsey said. "I've thought about that when I've been knocked down. You fall a lot in ski racing. Especially me."[8]

Maintaining Her Modesty

Skiing can indeed be a dangerous sport, particularly for skiers who like to ski fast. Lindsey quickly included herself in this group of skiers. By the age of ten, she had developed a burning desire to go faster and faster on the slopes at Buck Hill. Her ability to swoosh down hills faster than others never motivated her to boast, however. Although she gained tremendous confidence in her skiing, she stayed grounded. She understood that cockiness could hinder her performance. It also did not fit her personality. "She was never loud," Sailer said. "She was not a real showoff. She kept on plugging away. She was pushed by her father, and it worked. It surprised me. I did not know she would be that good."[9]

Neither did her competition. Lindsey did not make many friends among other skiers, most of whom were several years older. She was so much better than skiers her own age that she typically competed against older skiers. She was soon dominating those older skiers on the Buck Hill slopes, causing them great frustration. "I would finish a race and all the 14-year-olds at the bottom would be crying because a 10-year-old had beaten them,"[10] she recalls.

A Career Move

By that time Lindsey's parents believed their daughter was ready to take her talents and training to a higher level. Her father felt she needed to conquer much steeper slopes to learn how to win downhill competitions, which receive the most attention in the sport of skiing. The result was a move to Vail, Colorado, which is widely considered the center of the American skiing universe.

Lindsey was eleven years old when her mother drove her from Minnesota to Vail through a blinding blizzard. When Krohn wanted to stop, Lindsey insisted she could still see the lines on the road and that they should continue. Lindsey loved the trip she and her mother took. Krohn made the miles slip away by singing to her favorite rock music blaring from the tape player while her daughter rested in a sleeping bag in the backseat.

Although Lindsey was excited, the move to Vail had several downsides. Lindsey was separated from her four siblings and father, who needed to stay in Minnesota to practice law. The effect on her social life was also dramatic: Lindsey was separated from her friends in Burnsville, and it was hard for her to make new ones in Vail because she was homeschooled. "Vail was wonderful to me," she said, "but I missed all the traditional things of childhood—sleepovers, school dances, making friends in a conventional way." Although she was eventually reunited with the rest of her family, even that came at an emotional cost. "Halfway through the second season, the rest of the family also moved to Vail. Now all my brothers and sisters had left their friends for me," she said. "That was stressful on them. I felt so guilty."[11]

She has expressed thanks to her younger sister Karin, and triplet siblings, Dylan, Laura, and Reed, for accepting the move to Vail. She understands the sacrifices they made for her and that they had no choice in the matter (they were too young to contribute to the decision made by her parents). Yet they were forced to make new friends and adjust to new schools and surroundings. "It was hard for them," Lindsey said. "Vail's a real tight community. There aren't that many kids there. It wasn't an easy adjustment."[12]

Lindsey's mother set up a private law practice in Colorado. Alan remained in Minnesota and commuted to Vail only when

Vonn, right, attends the 2011 ESPY Awards with her sister Karin. Vonn has noted her appreciation for the sacrifices her siblings made so that their family could support her skiing career.

he could get away from his own work as an attorney. Lindsey, meanwhile, received her education through a distance learning course and was skiing all over the world. The time spent away from each other as a family was difficult for everyone.

Lindsey had asked her parents when she could return to her life in Burnsville. "My father didn't want to tell me until the ski

Picabo ... I See You

Among the most memorable and defining moments of Lindsey Vonn's childhood and skiing career occurred when she was ten, at a skate and ski shop near her Minnesota home. That was when she stood in line to meet Olympic skiing champion Picabo Street.

Picabo Street goes airborne during a downhill run at the 1994 Winter Olympics in Lillehammer, Norway.

Lindsey was brimming with excitement. She was thrilled to shake Street's hand and receive her autographed photo. Her own dreams of winning Olympic gold medals were strengthened by the experience. "When I first met [Street], it was a huge thrill and an unforgettable moment for me," she said years later. "She inspired me to become what I am today. If I can have even half that effect on some of the young athletes I come into contact with, it will be worth it."

Quoted in *Idaho Mountain Express and Guide.* "Lindsey Vonn Recalls Her Idol, Picabo Street." April 13, 2011. www.mtexpress.com/index2.php?ID=2005136117.

season was over, but they had sold the Minnesota house," she said. "That was the first time I realized just how far we were willing to go so I could be a ski racer. We uprooted everyone. I never did get to say goodbye to anyone in Minnesota."[13] Lindsey eventually accepted living in Vail and developed an appreciation of why the move was made. Her acceptance of it, however, took time. "We had built our dream home [in Minnesota]," she said. "All the kids' handprints are in the cement in the driveway. ... When you're young, you don't realize how much has to be sacrificed for something like this. Now, I appreciate everything my family did for me."[14]

Working to Reach Her Goals

Lindsey was enrolled at Ski Club Vail, an elite academy for budding winter-sport athletes. Despite the rigorous training and racing schedule, she embraced the opportunity to maximize her potential by working tirelessly. She refused to allow failure to slow her down. That became her philosophy in life and in skiing. "If you work hard, it will pay off in the end," she says. "When you fall down, just get up again. Setbacks help you concentrate. When successes fall into your lap, you lose sight of your goals."[15]

Lindsey set goals for herself even as a young teenager in Vail. She displayed enough talent to motivate her parents to send her to international competitions. At age fourteen she became the first American girl to win the Trofeo Topolino event in Italy, which is also known as "Junior Junior Worlds." Her name was etched alongside other young females who eventually won Overall World Cup titles. That victory earned her a spot on the U.S. ski team development squad, which trains the premier young skiers in the country. It is considered the first rung on the ladder to earning a spot on the Olympic team. It was a major step forward in her career and cemented her place as one of the most gifted young stars in the sport. She immediately impressed her fellow skiers with her sheer ability. "You could see right away, with her talent, she was going to be one of the top racers,"[16] said retired skier Kirsten Clark, a teammate for eight years.

Skiers make their way down a slope at the Vail Ski Club, where Vonn trained after moving to Colorado when she was eleven years old.

Lindsey soon started to compete in top-level youth events. She showed promise as early as November 1999 by twice placing in the top six in International Ski Federation slalom events in Colorado. (The International Ski Federation is better known by its name in French, Fédération Internationale de Ski, and is abbreviated FIS.) Slalom races are downhill ski competitions that require athletes to zigzag or wind their way through obstacles, such as flags. A month later she took second place in successive slalom Nor-Am (North American) Cup races in Canada. In April 2000 she captured her first gold medal by winning the giant slalom in an FIS race in Breckenridge, Colorado. Two months later in Vail she captured first in the slalom in another FIS competition.

In 1999 and 2000 she competed in the United States, Canada, Sweden, France, Switzerland, Germany, Austria, and Italy. A different event awaited her every week throughout the winter. Such a hectic international travel schedule paired with intense competition can prove traumatic to many teenagers. Lindsey's mother was aware of the possible pratfalls. She weighed the positives and negatives of allowing her daughter to travel and compete around the globe and decided to allow it. "She was 15, and it just kills you, because she had left home already," she said. "People say to me, 'How did you give up your child like that?' Lindsey wanted to be an Olympian. I gave her to the country. I saw it as a noble thing."[17] Greater triumphs were on the horizon. Unfortunately for Lindsey, so were obstacles in her personal life.

Chapter 2

Bumps on the Road to Stardom

Lindsey Kildow found the guilt she felt about causing her family to move from Minneapolis to Vail could be eased through competitive skiing. Her desire to maximize her talent and blossom into an Olympic champion allowed her to shut out mental and emotional distractions on the slopes. She achieved much during these years, yet she also encountered several bumps on the road to stardom.

Getting Better All the Time

Lindsey was improving in all four disciplines of skiing—slalom, downhill, giant slalom, and super G. She competed in two World Cup slalom races in 2000, though she crashed in one and failed to qualify in the other. She was ranked an impressive sixtieth in the world in the slalom at just fifteen years old.

In November 2000 she captured her first racing championship in the Super Series, a series of FIS competitions for top youth skiers aged fifteen and older. The event, which was held in the American skiing mecca of Aspen, Colorado, featured thirty-eight skiers. Lindsey clinched first place with a win in the super G. It was not until twenty other competitors swooshed down the mountain with slower times that she knew she had won, though. Until then she was forced to wait, watch, and hope nobody bested her time. "I was praying hard," she remembers. "I was pretty nervous."[18] Her youthful enthusiasm was on clear display as she jumped up and down to celebrate her victory. Wins would soon be harder to come by, however.

Advanced for Her Age

In 2000 and 2001 Lindsey skied in Europa Cup events, a level of racing that prepares top-level youth skiers for the World Cup circuit. Most top-level youth skiers stay on the Europa Cup during their mid-teens and do not compete on the World Cup circuit until they are eighteen or nineteen. Lindsey, however, advanced to World Cup competition when she was still only sixteen years old. While most other top-level sixteen-year-old skiers were competing in the Europa Cup, Lindsey was proving how advanced she was for her age by qualifying for World Cup events.

Sixteen-year-old Vonn, left, celebrates her third-place finish at the U.S. Alpine Championships at Big Mountain near Whitefish, Montana, in March 2001.

Though qualifying for World Cup events was a testament to her talent, it also placed her against many skiers who had had far more experience in top-level competition. The difference between her and the others in maturity in the sport concerned her, and she felt a bit overwhelmed by the older athletes. "I don't have the experience everyone else has," Lindsey said at the time. "This is their life; they've been doing it for God knows how long. I've only been doing it for a couple of years. For them it's all in a day's work, and it is for me, too, but in a different sense, because I haven't been doing it as long."[19]

She needed more experience in some of the races, particularly the super G and giant slalom. It had become apparent that she was far more comfortable in speed disciplines, such as the downhill, than in technical events, such as the giant slalom. Skill

The Alpine Skiing Events

The Winter Olympics feature four different skiing competitions. Among them are freestyle, cross-country, and Nordic, which combines ski jumping and cross-country. The most popular competition, however, is Alpine skiing, which consists of five separate events. They are downhill, slalom, giant slalom, super G, and super combined.

The downhill is run on the longest course. The skiers race virtually straight downhill only once. The skier with the fastest time earns the gold medal. The slalom is the shortest course and features sharp, quick twists and turns. The skiers race two separate courses on the same slope. The times are combined. The skier with the fastest combined time wins gold. The giant slalom follows the same format, but the turns are wider.

The super G, otherwise known as the super giant, is competed on a longer course than the slalom but shorter than the downhill. Only one run determines the winner. The super combined features one run each on two short courses. The times are combined to determine the champion.

gained from experience helps skiers truly shine in slalom competition. Lindsey was simply not experienced enough to win medals in those disciplines. But she soon began showing the potential to do just that.

The World Cup

Lindsey made her World Cup debut at a race in Park City, Utah, on November 18, 2000, although she did not have any notable performances throughout her first season. Rather than winning medals or placing in top spots, Lindsey spent this time gaining valuable experience and working on improving her skills. Although the top-tier international skiers overwhelmed her early in her World Cup career, she offered great promise in competition against young American skiers. She did not place in the top twenty-five in any World Cup event in the 2000–2001 season, though she did squeak by in twenty-fourth place in the super G in Switzerland in December 2001 (part of the 2001–2002 World Cup season). She fared better at home, where she placed third at the 2001 U.S. Championships in the combined competition, which includes two slalom runs and a downhill.

Lindsey was merely sixteen years old, yet she was displaying the all-around talents she had been developing since her childhood. She yearned to win multiple gold medals, which would require her to master all four disciplines. She was showing the versatility to at least compete in each of them. "I like slalom and downhill, and I'm getting better at giant slalom and super-G,"[20] she said after a November 2000 event in Colorado.

Lindsey discovered as her teenage years waned that it took intense training as well as tireless work on the slopes to maximize her potential. By the time she was seventeen, her hard work landed her a spot on the 2002 U.S. Olympic team. She had earned an opportunity to ski with and against the best in the world on the biggest stage. Her father was immensely proud of her, if not only to prove to critics that Lindsey had not been pushed into skiing, but sought these victories for herself. "It is impossible to push somebody to that level, impossible," he said

A seventeen-year-old Vonn poses for her official portrait as a member of the ski team representing the United States at the 2002 Winter Olympics in Nagano, Japan.

when his daughter made the team. "You cannot force people to get out of bed at 4:30 in the morning to train if they don't love it. … What we did is gave somebody with a lot of talent the opportunity to develop it."[21]

But the triumph of making the Olympic team was shadowed by a coinciding tragedy: As with past decisions and opportunities related to Lindsey's career, earning a spot on the Olympic team brought difficult changes for the Kildow family. The 1995 move from the Minneapolis suburbs to Vail had been tough on her parents' relationship, and their marriage had deteriorated in the years since. Seven years later, the same year Lindsey joined the Olympic team, her mother filed for divorce, which was finalized fourteen months later. Lindsey wondered whether the sacrifices her parents made to provide her with the best chance to succeed in skiing played a role in their ruined marriage. She expressed uncertainty over whether uprooting the family contributed to their eventual divorce. "I don't think my skiing was the reason, but it may have had something to do with it,"[22] she said.

First Olympic Experience

It was in the shadow of that divorce that Lindsey competed in the 2002 Winter Olympics in Salt Lake City, Utah. As she coped with her parents' separation, Lindsey was thrust into the international spotlight for the first time. Little was expected of her medal-wise because she was only seventeen years old, yet the media still took interest in the youngest member of the Olympic team. She responded to the scrutiny of and interest in her by forging ahead of her older and more experienced teammates and emerging as the most promising skier on the U.S. team.

The performance of most of the American women skiers in the February 2002 games was disappointing. None of Lindsey's teammates finished higher than eleventh in any event. Lindsey hoped to finish in the top ten. Her goal was to match or beat teammate Caroline Lalive's performance at the 1998 Olympics, in which she took seventh place in the combined, a competition which consists of one downhill and two slalom runs.

Vonn races down the slalom run of the women's combined event at the 2002 Winter Olympics in Salt Lake City, Utah, where the seventeen-year-old earned an impressive sixth-place finish.

To everyone's surprise, Lindsey outperformed Lalive and all the other American women. Although Lalive was considered a medal contender in the combined slalom, her hopes were dashed when she fell on the first run. Lindsey, meanwhile, launched her Olympic career by finishing a surprising eighth in the slalom. She followed with a fourth-place run in the downhill, the event in which she felt most comfortable. Her efforts earned her sixth place in the combined.

Lindsey expressed excitement but did not overstate her performance. "The slalom was OK," she said. "The first run, I had a pretty good run. I was excited about that. I was just trying to finish the second run, which I did. The downhill, all I wanted to do was put a really good run down, put it all on the line, and I did that."[23]

Amazed and Admiring

Those who watched Lindsey on the Salt Lake City slopes were far more complimentary than she was about her performance. Her performance opened the eyes of several people she needed to impress both professionally and personally. Among them was U.S. women's head coach Marjan Cernigoj. "Phenomenal," Cernigoj exclaimed about Lindsey's sixth-place finish. "Seventeen years old, first Olympics, we brought her here to get some experience, she gets this result—incredible."[24] Her father also expressed joy at his daughter's Olympic debut. "We are happy, very happy, happier than I could imagine," he said. "For one reason or another, she was very relaxed today and focused."[25]

Another person who was impressed with the young athlete was Aldo Radamus, who served as Alpine development director for the U.S. ski team. He said of Lindsey:

> From a very early age, she wanted to be, planned to be and prepared to be a ski racer at the highest level. She is very gifted in all of the skiing disciplines. She is very comfortable and very quick skiing slalom. She is very aggressive, always attacks slalom courses. She skis downhill the same way. She knows how to let the skis run, but how to properly attack a downhill course. That's a very rare skill in any ski racing athlete, but particularly one as young as her.[26]

Lindsey had little time to rest on her Olympic laurels. Within a week she was skiing in the FIS Junior World Championships in Europe, where she placed sixth and eleventh in two Junior World Championship races in Italy. She returned to the United States for more FIS competition and ended the 2002 season by finishing in the top eleven in three of four races. Though she was still not ready to establish herself as one of the premier skiers in the world, these successes boosted her confidence and helped make her performances more consistent.

Achieving a top-ten finish in the Salt Lake City Games, along with these other accomplishments, had Lindsey contemplating loftier goals. She set her sights on an eventual World Cup championship. "If I continue being good in all four events, I can win the (World Cup) overall [title] quite easily," she said. "In a couple of years it's going to come."[27]

Among those who saw great potential in Lindsey was fellow Olympic skier Thomas Vonn, whom she met during the 2002 Games. The two began dating despite the fact that she was nine years younger than him. Vonn made a profound impact on her

The Man Lindsey Loves

Although professionally Thomas Vonn has not enjoyed the same level of success on the slopes as his wife, he has valid, authoritative ski experience, and Lindsey has benefited from his advice and ideas.

Vonn was born December 3, 1975, in New York City. He learned to ski at the age of three at the Hunter Mountain Resort in the Catskill Mountains. "[He] possessed a natural touch for the snow," remembers Jim Catalano, who served as programs director at the Hunter Mountain Resort. Vonn began his racing career at the age of twelve. He trained at the Northwood School and the New York Ski Educational Foundation and

Vonn was a member of the United States ski team that competed at the 2002 Winter Olympics.

also attended St. Lawrence University. He eventually became a specialist in the giant slalom and super G with the U.S. Men's Ski Team.

Vonn peaked as a skier in the 2002 Winter Olympics in Salt Lake City, Utah. He placed ninth in the super G and nineteenth in the giant slalom. That was his last appearance in any Olympic competition.

Quoted in *New York Post*. "Champ Returns to Hunter Roots." December 20, 2002, p. 96.

personal life and also played a major role in convincing his young girlfriend of the importance of training outside the slopes. Although Lindsey had sacrificed much of her youth to establishing herself as one of the finest junior skiers in the country, her boyfriend understood that talent alone could only get her so far. Thomas Vonn realized it would take even more hard work—and definitely more intense training—to stand on the podium and accept a gold medal at an Olympic Games.

Memorable Bike Ride

That she needed to invest in a more vigorous and intense training regimen was driven home to Lindsey early in 2003 when she visited friend and junior skiing rival Julia Mancuso in Lake Tahoe, California. Lindsey joined Julia and her father on a long bicycle ride through the mountains. It was the kind of training necessary for young Olympic hopefuls, who require strength and endurance to blossom into champions. Lindsey felt ashamed when she could not keep up. "It was the first time I had ever done a bike ride, except for transportation around my little flat hometown in Minnesota," she said. "I fell way behind by, like, five miles, and I'm out in the middle of nowhere and Julia's beating me and I felt like a fool. I was totally embarrassed."[28]

Thomas Vonn used that humiliating event to convince her how important it was to train properly. He recalled the moment with clarity nearly a decade later. "That bike ride was kind of one of her first awakenings that she had," he said. "As an athlete, you kind of have these points where you realize what you've been doing probably wasn't good enough and you need to do more. That was certainly one of those times where she was like, 'OK, Julia is my competition and she dropped me on a bike ride. I have no chance against her. How am I going to beat her in a ski race? I've got to change something here.'"[29]

The bike ride with Julia forced Lindsey to rethink her approach to training. She began working out six weeks a year with professional trainer Jacques Choynowski at his Monaco home. Choynowski was the former coach of the Polish swimming team

Vonn's intensified training regimen resulted in a bronze medal at a World Cup event in January 2004 in Cortina d'Ampezzo, Italy.

and had made his mark as a personal trainer for premier Olympic athletes. The arrangement lasted three years and paid off immediately. Under Choynowski's tutelage, Lindsey became leaner and gained speed on the slopes. She credited him with improving her conditioning and shape. "My body changed," she said. "I got rid of my baby fat."[30] As a result of her intense training, she earned her first World Cup medal in January 2004, taking the bronze in Cortina d'Ampezzo, Italy. She blossomed into a consistent contender in Junior World Ski competitions while displaying her versatility. In one February 2004 event in Slovenia, for example, she placed second in the downhill, fourth in the super G, third in the giant slalom, and fourth in the combined.

Deteriorating Relationship with Dad

Although Lindsey's growing romance with Thomas Vonn improved her competitive performance, it worsened her relationship with her father, which was already crumbling. Alan Kildow did not approve of his daughter's courtship with a man nine years her senior. The strain in the bond between father and daughter, as well as the relationship between Lindsey and Thomas, went beyond personal feelings. It extended into her career and working relationship with her skiing coaches.

The problems between the two men in Lindsey's life soon began to affect her professional relationship with her coaches. Both Alan Kildow and Thomas Vonn had taken it upon themselves to play a role in Lindsey's career, which her coaches did not appreciate. The coaches complained that Kildow was trying to execute his own training regimen for his daughter, which conflicted with their agenda. Meanwhile, Vonn was serving as an unofficial skiing instructor. *New York Times* writer Bill Pennington summed up the situation. "Her coaches confided in me at the time that [Lindsey] was struggling with a complex personal situation," he wrote. "Just where Thomas fit in was a conundrum for the coaches ... because he had begun acting as a tutor. Nor were the coaches pleased with Alan Kildow."[31]

Lindsey felt that her father's professional guidance had turned into a hindrance. "Obviously, my dad knew what was right for me for a long time,' she said. "I liked and appreciated it then, but it was intense. When I got to the U.S. ski team and I was older, his input wasn't helping anymore; it was tearing me down. It was negative. I was reaching a breaking point."[32]

Vonn sought opportunities to strengthen his relationship with Kildow and gain his acceptance. He understood it was natural for a father to be concerned about a nine-year age difference between a young daughter and her boyfriend. But he could not understand why Kildow did not make a greater attempt to talk to him or get to know him. "I can see any father being upset at the age difference," Vonn said. "But I would at least try to meet the person and have a dialogue."[33] Lindsey, meanwhile, did not believe she should be forced to choose between maintaining a relationship with the man she was falling in love with and pleasing her father. "I loved him," Lindsey said about Thomas. "And I didn't want to end my relationship just because [my father] said so. It forced me to take sides."[34]

The conflict between her boyfriend and father came at a time when Lindsey was trying to maximize her potential as a ski racer and was one of several key obstacles she faced in her life and career. Another obstacle was her need for speed on the slopes, which would lead to crashes and injuries that would test her resolve and frustrate her in her quest for Olympic gold.

Chapter 3

Falling, Recovering, Winning

Lindsey Kildow did not have a second gear when skiing competitively until Thomas Vonn convinced her to tone down her breakneck style a bit. Through most of her career, she embraced a go-for-broke approach that helped her blossom into an Olympic champion, but also brought a sense of danger to her racing. This style has resulted in several accidents that have knocked her out of competition for weeks or more at a time, but it has also made her famous as a skier who goes all out, all the time.

A Taste for Speed

One of Lindsey's first notable crashes occurred when she was eighteen years old, in December 2002 at Lake Louise in Alberta, Canada. She came off the top of a slope on a hill, hooked the tip of her ski, and went down. The tumble caused a severe strain of the hip flexor muscles in her left leg. She was escorted off the mountain and to the hospital by helicopter. "It was pretty bad," she said. "I thought I had ripped my leg off."[35] The injury did not require surgery, but it knocked her out of action for a month.

It seemed that no fall could deter Lindsey from going full bore on the slopes, however. By the end of 2003 a style of skiing some called reckless was giving her multiple first-place finishes outside of more challenging World Cup competition. It was an aspect of her personality that her father appreciated, even though

Vonn goes airborne as she speeds past a gate during a downhill run at the U.S. Alpine Championships at Whiteface Mountain in Wilmington, New York, in March 2003. Her all-out, sometimes reckless style has resulted in both impressive finishes and injuries.

his own career had been cut short by a knee injury suffered in a skiing accident. "The ability to hold the throttle down when most reasonable people would let up on the throttle—Lindsey has that,"[36] he said. Buck Hill coach Erich Sailer, who was familiar with the skiing techniques of both father and daughter, described Lindsey's taste for speed in the following way: "As a racer, she is like her father. She would rather be dead than not succeed."[37]

Lindsey delivered impressive performances even as she sustained injuries. For example, in Alyeska, Alaska, during the 2004 National Championships that concluded the World Cup season, she took second-place silver in the downhill in an FIS race. She then snagged the gold in both the super G and slalom

Bovine for Lindsey

After winning a downhill race in Val d'Isère, France, in 2005, Lindsey was given the choice of taking the prize money or a cow. The option was presented to her as a joke. But Lindsey was not joking when she chose the cow. She named the bovine Olympe in honor of the upcoming Olympic Games in Italy.

Vonn poses with Olympe, a cow that she won at a downhill race in France in 2005.

Lindsey's animal family has been growing ever since on a farm just outside the French town of Kirchberg. In the fall of 2006, Olympe gave birth to a female whom Lindsey called Sunny because she wanted it to have a bright and fun name. Two years later Olympe produced another female calf that Lindsey named Karin after her own younger sister. "At the time, [sister] Karin wasn't too psyched about it," Lindsey said. "But now she thinks it's pretty funny. If you've ever seen my sister, you'd know she's not even close to a cow. She's gorgeous." In 2009 Olympe and Sunny each gave birth. Those calves were named Shirley and Don after Lindsey's grandparents.

Lindsey's animal collection does not stop at cows. During a celebration after Lindsey won two gold medals in Val d'Isère in 2009, the town of Kirchberg gave her a goat, which she named Laura after another sister. She has said that if she could own any exotic animal, it would be a baby cheetah, which probably will not be added to her collection any time soon.

Quoted in U.S. Ski and Snowboard. "Vonn's Other Family Tree Began in Val d'Isere." December 17, 2009. http://skiing.teamusa.org/news/2009/12/17/vonn-s-other-family-tree-began-in-val-d-isere/29979.

in the National Championships at the same venue. She finished the event and the season by taking sixth in the giant slalom. Most remarkable was that she earned these medals despite a fall that left her with a minor concussion, a cut on her chin, and an aching back. She did not even know if she would be able to compete because her mind was a bit groggy. "I was worried if I'd remember the course,"[38] she said.

When Lindsey was not sidelined by injury, she was proving to be one of the most promising young skiers in the world. But one never knew which Lindsey would show up. She sprinkled in brilliant, dominating performances between crashes and inconsistency. She competed well in FIS events but did not consistently match the talent and experience of her opponents in the World Cup.

"I Could Probably Compete Until I Die"

Lindsey's desire to win multiple Olympic gold medals led her to race in all four disciplines in both juniors and World Cup competition (she was still young enough to compete with the juniors, and ambitiously chose to compete in both circuits). It was a grueling challenge, but one that reflected her determination and motivation.

While the older skiers received a rest when the World Cup schedule allowed a week off, she was swooshing downhill in youth competitions. The downhill and super G were her best events. She was also gaining tremendous experience in the slalom and giant slalom. By 2004 she was beginning to be seen as a contender for a gold medal in the upcoming 2006 Olympics. "She's having a tremendous year," said U.S. Ski Team Alpine director Jesse Hunt. "She has obviously made a huge breakthrough on the World Cup in downhill. She's established herself in the speed events and used that confidence to start scoring in all disciplines. She established herself as one of our up-and-comers, but now she's turning that potential into results."[39]

Lindsey was starting to be seen as the heir apparent to Picabo Street, who had retired in 2002. The U.S. team was looking for

Vonn celebrates her victory in the slalom event at the 2004 U.S. Alpine Championships at Alyeska Resort in Alaska, one of a string of successful performances that set her up for a spot on the 2006 Winter Olympic team.

a young woman with the same potential. Lindsey knew that the expectations for her were growing with every World Cup triumph, and she was enjoying the ride. "I'm having a great time," she said in February 2004. "I just like competing. I could probably compete until I die."[40]

Reckless or Just Aggressive?

Some worried Lindsey *could* die while competing. Her love for downhill racing was based on her desire to travel as fast as possible on the slopes regardless of risk. She exhibited a sense of fearlessness in the twists and turns of slalom events despite the obvious danger.

Yet Lindsey did not consider herself to be reckless. She believed her style was based on a simple strategy: the faster you ski, the better chance you have to win. She was willing to chance a crash in her attempt to win races. The bumps, bruises, and occasional injuries, in her opinion, simply came with the territory. She thought if she held correct form (position), she could avoid injury no matter how fast she went and beat more conservative skiers in the process. "You have to be technically sound when you're going fast; if you don't you're going to crash," she says. "If there is bravery it's in having the speed but not thinking about how quickly you're travelling, or how badly you would hurt yourself if you fell. That sort of thing can get into your head and play tricks on you." Ultimately, Lindsey thinks that going fast is just part and parcel of skiing. "Extreme sports seem to be what everyone's into now," she explains. "Well, this is the original extreme sport. In Downhill I'm going 90 miles an hour and getting 40 meters of air [underneath her when she jumps]. It's a lot and it does require courage."[41]

Test of Courage

Lindsey's philosophy was put to the test in Italy in early February 2005. She hurt her back and wrist during a training run for the World Ski Championships. The accident occurred after she skied

Vonn slides across the finish line after a fall at the World Ski Championships in Santa Caterian Valfurva, Italy, in February 2005. Despite injuries suffered during an earlier training run, she remained in the competition.

out of control. She twisted into the air and landed backward. She fell on her back and spun on the ground several times as she hurtled down the hard, icy snow. Lindsey sped down the course and slammed into a group of photographers.

She could have nursed her injuries and begged out of the event, but her competitive side would not allow it. In typical Lindsey Kildow fashion, she shrugged off the severity of her injuries. "I'm lucky," she exclaimed. "I just banged myself up a little bit. I've got a nice bruise on my back. I broke my pole and it hurts on my right hand where the grip goes. But I'll be going at 'em tomorrow."[42]

She maintained an aggressive approach throughout the World Championships, even though she finished a disappointing ninth in the giant slalom. She cried over the poor performance and said she was affected in part by the media attention and scrutiny that comes with budding stardom. "I'm just really sad," she said after the giant slalom run. "To have so many expectations … but that's ski racing. All the media attention, I'm not used to it. But I have to learn to deal with it. I have to analyze what I did wrong [in the race] and what I did wrong in my head and try to change it."[43]

Lindsey won the third-place bronze medal in the downhill in the combined disciplines and placed fourth in the overall downhill and combined. That might have been good enough for many young skiers, but not for her. She had planned on winning those events and was deeply disappointed when she did not.

Falling Out with Father

The media speculated that Lindsey's intensifying feud with her father played a role in the disappointing performance in Italy. Alan Kildow had continued to criticize her courtship with Thomas Vonn, which grew in intensity by the year. Vonn retired from racing in 2005, which freed him up to become more involved in his girlfriend's professional life. Lindsey resented her father's disapproval of their relationship and also the fact that he was negative when she performed poorly. "[My father] always supported me when I did well, which was 90 percent of the time," she explained. "But when I didn't, he didn't handle it very well. It was so hot and cold. It was so much criticism and so much negativity, and it was really hard to balance my emotions."[44]

After several intense arguments with her father over her relationship with Thomas and the direction of her career, Lindsey decided to end all communication with Alan Kildow. "It was a buildup of many things, and I felt pushed over the edge," she told an inquiring reporter. No one will ever know exactly what happened to sever their relationship except for Lindsey and Alan. But in Lindsey's mind, the estrangement was more than justified. "It might seem strange or harsh, [but] it is just something I had to do to make my life more stable."[45]

Her father has admitted over the years to the rift with his daughter but has refused to go into detail outside of the fact that he disapproved of her dating an older man. He has continued to express pride in her achievements on the slopes. Lindsey maintained a strong relationship with her mother, who approved of her feelings for Vonn, and to her paternal grandparents.

The Turin Crash

As her relationships with her father and Vonn went in opposite directions, the 2006 Olympics crept closer. But Lindsey was not skiing like a gold medalist. The distractions in her personal life played a role in her mediocre and inconsistent performance in World Cup events that preceded the 2006 Winter Games in Turin, Italy.

In December 2005, for example, she won an event at Lake Louise, Canada, to become the first American woman to take first in a World Cup race in successive years since Picabo Street accomplished the feat a decade earlier. That same month she won the downhill and finished fourth in the super G in an event in

Vonn arrives via helicopter at a hospital in Turin, Italy, after a crash during a downhill training run at the 2006 Winter Olympics. She was back on the racing course two days later.

Sneaking Out of the Hospital

Lindsey's tremendous desire to get back to the slopes after crashing and injuring herself in a training run for the 2006 Winter Games was overwhelming. She yearned to complete her Olympic training. Her emotional need so overwhelmed any other thoughts about recovery that she even tried to sneak out of the hospital.

During her stay at the trauma center in Turin, Italy, she snuck down the hallway toward the elevator in her hospital gown. But as soon as the elevator doors opened, a group of nurses appeared from around the corner and stopped her from leaving the grounds. She was not released until the next day.

France. But she followed these shining moments by placing no better than tenth in the next ten races. Although she recovered to finish third in a super combined in Switzerland and in a super G in Italy, she was clearly distracted by off-slope personal tensions. These tensions might have also played a role in a critical and violent crash she suffered just days before the Olympics.

During an Olympic training run in Turin, she caught her ski on the snow three-quarters of the way down the course. She was traveling about 70 miles an hour (113kph) and twisted out of control, 15 feet (4.6m) into the air. She landed hard on the left side of her pelvis with her legs spread awkwardly while her head slammed into the ground. She was escorted off the slope by toboggan and taken by helicopter to the hospital.

Doctors feared she had broken her back. Vonn thought at least one knee and possibly both had been torn up. He was certain her Olympic dreams were over, at least for 2006. Friend and former gold medal skier Picabo Street stayed with her in the hospital to buoy her spirits, but not much could soothe Lindsey's physical pain. "Imagine a sledgehammer hitting you in the pelvis without breaking anything,"[46] said ski team physician Bill Sterett of what Lindsey's injuries must have felt like.

Despite excruciating pain in her back, she raced two days later. Any legitimate shot at a medal was gone, but she did manage to place eighth in the downhill. Ski fans and even casual observers who knew little about the sport and only watched during the Olympics marveled that she competed at all. "She's tougher than I am, if you can imagine that," said Street, who returned from leg and knee injuries to take gold in the 1998 Games. Added Sterett: "I've known Lindsey for about 10 years. She's a pretty tough young lady. Almost nothing surprises me about her."[47] Olympians and media members recognized Lindsey's perseverance by presenting her with the U.S. Olympic Spirit Award.

Trying to Turn a Negative into a Positive

Although her tenacity had impressed onlookers, Lindsey was depressed that the crash in Turin had destroyed her chance to win Olympic gold. After all, the Winter Games roll around just once every four years. Athletes have but two shots per decade to make their Olympic mark; if they miss their opportunity, they must wait four years and may find themselves out of peak condition by the time another Olympics occurs. The sense of loss can be overwhelming. So can the knowledge that four more years of training and competition must be completed before the next Olympics.

The feeling of losing this short window of opportunity haunted Lindsey in late 2006. She knew she could train to compete in 2010, but it seemed an eternity away. She lamented:

It bums me out—you see everyone else has had success at the Olympics and is pretty much set for life. Everyone recognizes them as Olympic champions. I really wanted that. I wanted that since I was a little kid. It was definitely hard, and it's going to be hard until the next Olympics. I'm just going to have to stay positive, keep my goals at the front of my head and try to take advantage of the time I have right now—the World Cup, the World Championships, and wait for my moment.[48]

Ultimately, Lindsey did not let the lost opportunity defeat her. Over time she gained a stronger desire to accomplish her goals. "That [crash] happened for a reason," she said. "It was a missed opportunity, but it gave me the fuel and motivation that I needed."[49]

Lindsey showed that motivation by intensifying her training program and embarking on the finest run of performances of her career to that point. She snagged a gold medal in the super G in a World Cup event in Norway just a month after the Olympics concluded. Lindsey was soon ready to become a consistent champion.

Grabbing the Gold

When Lindsey took her life-changing bike ride with Julia Mancuso in 2003, she simply could not keep up. By the summer of 2006, however, she was armed with a new sense of purpose, a determination not to miss another Olympic opportunity, and was about to embark on a new training regime. She was determined to transform herself into a gold-medal seeking machine. For Lindsey, both eyes were on the 2010 Olympics in Vancouver, Canada. In the four years until that ultimate competition, she continued to hone her skills, work on her control, and give her sport all she had.

A New Workout Regimen

Sponsored by the energy drink company Red Bull, Lindsey embarked on a new training program headed by legendary Austrian skiing coach Robert Trenkwalder and trainer Martin Hager. Like many observers, Hager had noted Lindsey's wild, even reckless, skiing style. He thought he could help her maximize her performance by whipping her into peak shape; this would help her control her body and thus avoid injury, even as she raced down the slope at breakneck speed. "I saw that she raced very aggressively," he said. "I would say, 'This girl is crazy.' She didn't have the conditioning and stability to take such risks."[50] The program he and Trenkwalder designed for Lindsey had her spending up to six weeks every year in Austria for an intense workout regimen that focused on endurance.

Vonn does an agility exercise during a workout. Her commitment to intense training programs to improve her strength and stamina has allowed her to maximize her performance.

The regimen consisted of four-hour-long morning sessions that tested her strength and stamina. In the afternoon she spent three hours riding a stationary bike. It took a lot of time and hard work. The intensity of her workouts sometimes angered Lindsey, who would show her frustration by screaming, "I hate you!"[51] to Hager. But she eventually showed stamina on the same kind of mountain bike on which she was embarrassed trying to keep up with Julia Mancuso several years earlier. After several years of this grueling training, she had no problem keeping up with Hager and accomplished cyclist and skier Fritz Strobl on a 3-mile (4.8km) ascent up an Austrian mountain.

Scorching the Slopes

The help she received from her new trainers proved worthwhile. Hager and Oliver Saringer, who also worked as a physical therapist, started traveling with her to supervise her on the World Cup circuit, where Lindsey wasted no time displaying her dominance. She captured gold medals in back-to-back giant slalom runs in FIS races in Japan in August 2006. She maintained her momentum when World Cup events rolled around late that fall. At Lake Louise, in Canada, she placed first in one downhill run, second in another, and second in the super G. Not only was she making frequent visits to the podium to collect medals, she was also earning them in a variety of disciplines.

The trend continued as the holiday season approached. In December 2006 she won a downhill event in France. Lindsey then celebrated the new year by snagging two silver medals in Austria, a gold and silver in Italy and two silvers in the FIS World Ski Championships in Sweden. She placed second in the downhill despite faltering at the top of the course. In showing how she had matured as a skier, Lindsey was winning medals and competitions without sacrificing her breakneck style. "If you're trying to win you know you have to risk everything," she said. She explained her downhill win in the following way. "I pretty much just threw reason out the window. I turned my brain off ... and just went for it. I was pretty much on auto-pilot at that point."[52]

Vonn proudly displays the two silver medals she won at the FIS World Ski Championships in Sweden in February 2007.

Getting Down in the Downhill

The new year had brought other kinds of gold and silver into Lindsey's life: On New Year's Eve 2006, she and Thomas Vonn got engaged, and the couple was married nine months later, in September 2007. As her husband, Thomas worked with her to temper her aggressiveness on the slopes to minimize risks, and this approach paid off as Lindsey became one of the premier World Cup performers during the 2007–2008 season.

Lindsey Vonn was virtually unbeatable in the downhill, finishing no lower than fifth in dozens of downhill races throughout the season. She placed first in that event at Lake Louise in early December 2007 and matched those efforts in Austria, Italy, and Switzerland. As the year progressed she improved in the super G, slalom, and giant slalom, too. She finished fourth in the super G in Italy and Switzerland and sixth in the giant slalom in Italy and Germany. By mid-March she had clinched her first overall World Cup championship. "These titles are not easy to come by," Vonn said. "It's really an amazing accomplishment."[53]

Vonn races in an FIS World Cup event in St. Moritz, Switzerland, in December 2008, capping a stretch in which she demonstrated her versatility beyond downhill events.

Ski Switch

Lindsey Vonn took a bit of a risk during the 2010 World Cup season when she switched from women's skis to men's skis in competition. She began using them in both the downhill and super G events.

The men's skis provide more stability at high speeds, which both she and her husband consider to be a huge advantage. They also proved to be safer for Vonn, who earned a reputation for taking chances on the slopes.

Although talented rivals such as Maria Riesch and Anja Parson of Sweden experimented with men's skis with mixed results, the skis worked well for Vonn. "I'm taller and maybe a little bit heavier than most of the other girls," Vonn said. "So for me, the men's skis are more stable. It's hard to turn, of course, it takes more strength. But I'm able to generate a lot of speed from the turns."

Quoted in Associated Press. "Vonn's Secret to Success? Men's Skis." *San Francisco Chronicle*, December 19, 2009. http://articles.sfgate.com/2009-12-19/sports/17331786_1_super-combined-lindsey-vonn-world-cup.

Vonn was ready to shine when the National Championships in Maine rolled around in late March. She won gold in the slalom, silver in the downhill, and nearly captured a bronze in the super G. By the time she skied her last course in 2008, she had shown medal-winning potential in not just downhill, but in the other events as well.

Gold, Gold, and More Gold

Vonn had one more season to perfect her skills before the 2010 Winter Olympics in Vancouver. In the 2008–2009 season, she did just that. It was mission accomplished in the 2009 World Cup competition. She proved to be the dominant skier throughout the season. She became virtually unstoppable by midwinter. From one

Vonn, center, celebrates her gold-medal victory in the super G at the podium after winning the super G race at the FIS World Ski Championships in France in February 2009.

event in Germany in late January to the National Championships in Alaska two months later, she won ten gold medals and added two silvers and a bronze. Not only did she dominate the downhill competitions, she also earned frequent firsts in other events. She won the super combined in Austria in March 2009, for example. That same month she ended the season by capturing gold in the super G in Germany, Sweden, and Bulgaria and also won gold in the slalom in Germany, Finland, and National Championships in Alaska.

Her peak performance that season occurred at the World Ski Championships in France in February 2009. Vonn won both the super G and downhill during that two-week event. She overwhelmed the same international field against which she would compete in the Olympics. Vonn was now the anticipated winner in just about any World Cup race. "My goal was to win the world downhill and I'm thrilled at pulling through," she said after dominating that discipline in France. "Today was a dream-come-true for me."[54]

Another dream came true weeks later when she sealed her second consecutive overall World Cup championship. She became the first American to accomplish the feat. When asked about it by members of the media, she became philosophical. She spoke about all she had surrendered in her personal life to become a back-to-back champion. "I didn't go to prom, I didn't go to a regular high school for a year," she said. "I sacrificed all these things for skiing." She added that she was now setting her sights on the 2010 Winter Olympics in Vancouver, Canada. "[The Olympics] mean everything. The overall [World Cup] titles have been incredible, and they're something you work extremely hard for. But the Olympics are very special. I hope the Olympics will give me a chance to show people who I am, and the sport I love."[55]

Lofty Expectations

As the 2010 Winter Olympics approached, U.S. Ski Team members and foreign foes alike spoke glowingly about Vonn. For example, U.S. teammate Jonna Mendes complimented Vonn's flawless form. "In speed events most skiers are either gliders, who try to gain time on the flat sections, or technical skiers, who turn well and try not to lose too much on the flats," Mendes explained. "Picabo Street was a great skier, but she was a glider. Lindsey isn't just one, she's both. She can build a lead by gliding on the flats and then nail the technical sections too. It's a huge advantage. She has no weakness."[56] Even Vonn's competition, German skier Maria Riesch, said, "I'm sure she'll win medals."[57]

Mendes and Riesch were among the many who predicted Vonn would make a huge impact on the skiing competition in the Vancouver Games. They needed no crystal balls to forecast such success. Vonn raised everyone's expectations by snagging gold in eleven World Cup races leading up to the Olympics. Included in these was a back-to-back gold medal performance in France and a three-race sweep in a January event in Austria. She showed her increasing versatility by being particularly dominant in the downhill and super G.

Accident *Off* the Slopes

Lindsey Vonn is not only accident prone while skiing, she has even hurt herself celebrating her skiing triumphs. In early February 2009 Vonn was at a party to celebrate winning the downhill event at the World Ski Championships in France when a party guest opened a bottle of champagne with the edge of a ski, breaking the top of it in the process.

Vonn's hand and arm are immobilized by a splint following surgery to repair a severed tendon in her thumb in February 2009.

Not realizing there were sharp, jagged edges, Vonn cut the tendon of her right thumb when she grabbed the bottle to spray champagne over the guests. The injury required surgery and four stitches. "[What] was supposed to be a wonderful night turned into total chaos," she said.

Vonn could not compete in the giant slalom but did return to race in the slalom three days later. Despite being hampered by the injury, she took two gold medals in Italy in the next World Cup event.

Quoted in Philip Hersh. "Lindsay Vonn Hopes to Ski with Injured Thumb." *Chicago Tribune*, February 13, 2009. http://articles.chicagotribune.com/2009-02-13/sports/0902120973_ 1_lindsey-vonn-slalom-world-cup.

The Winter Games

As the games approached, however, Vonn was eerily reminded of the dream-crushing injury that had dashed her hopes of medaling at the 2006 Olympics. On February 2, 2010—just eleven days before the opening ceremonies of the Vancouver

A delighted Vonn holds the American flag after winning gold in the downhill event at the 2010 Winter Olympics in Vancouver, Canada.

Olympics—Vonn sustained another injury on another training run. This time, she smashed her shin so badly that she could barely walk, let alone ski. "She couldn't even put on ski boots without wincing in pain,"[58] noted Brian Gomez in the *Colorado Springs Gazette*. Vonn feared that, for the second time in her career, injury would prevent her from participating in the Games at her fullest.

Vonn was not about to let this chance slip away. She managed three days of skiing practice despite throbbing pain in her shin. She spread numbing cream on the bruise to ease the agony. Her gutsy attitude impressed U.S. Ski Team women's coach Jim Tracy. "She's a fighter," he said. "I knew 100 percent, whether she was going to be sore or not, she was going to be ready to race."[59]

That she did. She needed a swift run in the downhill to beat teammate Julia Mancuso, who set a fast pace. Vonn scorched the course. She hit a bump and appeared to lose her balance at the bottom, but her time of 1 minute 44.19 seconds proved more than a half second faster than that of Mancuso. After almost a lifetime of skiing and nearly fifteen years of competition and training, Vonn won her first Olympic gold medal.

The triumph in the face of injury thrilled onlookers, who had feared for the fate of the wounded skier. "Hurt shin? What hurt shin?" quipped *People's* Steve Daly. "The endorsement-ready poster girl for Vancouver 2010 has arrived, and she's not limping."[60] Brian Gomez of the *Colorado Springs Gazette* agreed. "Lindsey Vonn sure knows how to shake off an injury," he wrote. "She's also becoming pretty skilled at etching her name in the Alpine skiing record books."[61] Of the athlete's long-coveted medal, Bleacher Report's Ash Marshall said, "I guess you could say it was just what the doctor ordered."[62] But of all the onlookers, none was prouder than her husband, who said, "The Olympics are the ultimate numbing cream."[63]

As for Vonn, she was relieved, happy, and satisfied. "A huge weight has been lifted off my shoulders," she said. She cried for twenty minutes upon seeing her name occupy the number one spot. "I got the gold medal I came here to get. And now I'm going to attack every day, with no regrets and no fear. And, I mean, I'm just happy with one. Anything else from here on out is a bonus."[64]

That bonus came in the form of a bronze medal in the super G. Unfortunately, her penchant for crashes came back to haunt her in the giant slalom when she hit a bump, spun into a gate and broke a finger. She performed poorly the rest of the Games.

It mattered little to the American public and media. Writing for the *New York Times*, Bill Pennington called Vonn's gold-medal run "one of the most stirring descents in Olympic downhill skiing history."[65] Canadian skier Emily Brydon said of Vonn, "She's superhuman. She did what any athlete strives for: ... to be there when the moment calls for it and everybody is watching. I think she's going to mark her spot in history."[66] As the first U.S. woman to win the Olympic downhill, Vonn became the darling of the 2010 Winter Games. *Seattle Times* sports columnist Ron Judd dubbed her "inarguably the greatest skier ever from America,"[67] while Gannett news service's Mike Lopresti described the victory in the following way: "In the middle of it all, [there is] the golden girl with the throbbing shin, who did what great champions must do."[68]

"It Doesn't Get Much Better"

Vonn was back on the slopes a mere one week after the Olympics ended, and before the 2010 season was over, she had even more historic wins under her belt. In the weeks that followed the Vancouver Olympics, Vonn finished four races in World Cup competition. She took gold in both a downhill event in Switzerland and a super G in Germany. She added silver medals in those same disciplines before the season finally ended. These triumphs gave her the World Cup title for the year in both events and made her the most decorated World Cup skier in American history, with thirty-three gold medals. In her trademark accident-prone style, these wins were not without injury: she had a bruised right knee from falling in the giant slalom and was still nursing the bruised shin and broken right finger from the Olympics. But she decided to race anyway, and the decision paid off.

Vonn also captured the overall World Cup title for the third consecutive year. She was overwhelmed with all she had achieved in 2010. "This was the dream season," she said. "To break the U.S. record in World Cup wins and to get the Olympic gold in the downhill, my favorite discipline, and the overall title for the third time, for me it doesn't get much better."[69]

Chapter 5

When the Skis Come Off

In the wake of her historic Olympic win, Lindsey Vonn found it almost impossible to escape the spotlight. "After I won my medal, I went home for 10 minutes," she said. "I've been moving continuously since then. I get tired, but it's … been a fun ride, for sure."[70] Eventually, however, life quieted down for the star skier, and she was able to spend some time off the slope doing the activities she loves with the people she treasures.

Mr. Lindsey

The person closest to Lindsey Vonn is her husband, Thomas, whom the media occasionally calls "Mr. Lindsey." After living together for four years, the couple married on September 29, 2007. One might think a woman who has made a career of careening down icy mountains at tremendous speeds would not be nervous on her wedding day. But the soon-to-be Lindsey Vonn was terrified.

Lindsey experienced what she described as a panic attack at her wedding at the Silver Lake Lodge in Deer Valley, Utah. Yet in the same way Thomas has helped her remain cool and collected on the slopes, he helped calm her on one of the most important days in her life. "I was hyperventilating," she remembers. "Thomas was whispering, 'breath, breath.' I felt like I was going to pass out, or start crying."[71]

Vonn kisses her husband, Thomas, after winning the super G race at the FIS World Ski Championships in France in February 2009. The couple married in 2007.

After the wedding, Lindsey was able to relax and enjoy the party. The dinner table was decorated with centerpieces named after prominent ski racing venues, such as Vail and Beaver Creek. The 140 guests feasted on steak, chicken, and black forest chocolate cake. Absent from the guest list was Lindsey's father, who objected to the marriage and to whom she was no longer speaking. When asked by *New York Times* reporter Bill Pennington if she felt sad that the man who first put her on a ski slope was not there to share in her happiness, Lindsey simply said, "That's his fault."[72] She was escorted down the aisle instead by her paternal grandfather.

The couple had little trouble adjusting to married life. Just three weeks after the wedding, Lindsey realized that she and Thomas had grown even closer. "There's more unity and a connection we didn't have before,"[73] she said. Lindsey had always good-naturedly called Thomas by his last name. That did not change after they were married, even though they now shared that name. In interviews she sometimes confuses reporters by talking about "Vonn and I,"[74] by which she means herself and her husband.

Making Medaling Look Good

Not only does Lindsey Vonn make winning a gold medal look easy, she also looks good while doing it. Reportedly, the star athlete wears makeup while she skis. In an interview with FanHouse's Will Brinson, Vonn described her slope-side makeup regimen:

> I pretty much don't go anywhere without putting makeup on—I just feel better about myself. And ski-racing is tough because it's not like other sports; you know, like tennis, for example, you can do your sport, take a shower and then you do your interviews. When we get down from the hill, we give interviews and what you have for that race is what you have for the entire day. So for me, I feel better and more comfortable with makeup on, so why not?

Quoted in AOL News. "Lindsey Vonn Talks Gold Medals, Her Injury and Skiing with Makeup." March 19, 2010. www.aolnews.com/2010/03/19/lindsey-vonn-talks-gold-medals-her-injury-and-skiing-with-makeu.

The Husband-Wife Team

As her husband, Thomas Vonn's influence on Lindsey's skiing career has been critical. Although he had served as a coach for her for two years while they dated, once they married, the rest of her team allowed him an authority they had previously denied him. "I was no longer just some yahoo boyfriend,"[75] he said. Becoming family gave him an all-access pass to everything related to Lindsey's career.

Just as Lindsey had given all her trust to her father as a young girl, she gave all her trust to Thomas as an adult. Lindsey has used her husband for emotional support on the slopes. She has a tendency to get nervous before major events, and Thomas has proved instrumental

The Vonns review details of a slalom ski run togerther before a race in Aspen, Colorado, in November 2008. Thomas provides Lindsey with both technical instruction and emotional support as she pursues her racing career.

in helping her stay calm. During the downhill competition of the World Ski Championships in France in February 2009, for example, she was so distraught that she radioed Thomas at the bottom of the mountain and begged him to come up. He joined her, made a few jokes, and gave her encouragement. She ended up winning the race by more than a half second. Thomas aims to play a wide-ranging role in his wife's professional life. "My role can be anything, whatever she needs," he once said. "Normally, I'm in a coaching role. But that can switch very quickly to emotional support."[76]

Thomas not only understands how to deal with his wife's emotions and nerves, he also boasts a strong feel for the sport, having been an Olympic skier in his own right. He is therefore in an excellent position to give his wife tips about equipment and how to handle or approach various venues. "At first I found it difficult to read courses or understand slopes," Lindsey says. "Thomas was a huge help when it came to inspecting the courses."[77] Thomas also plays a role in the training program that made her more fit. His wife appreciates all of it. "Thanks to Thomas, I can focus entirely on my sport," Lindsey says. "He comes to all my races, he can console me, motivate me or take my mind off things when it's not going so well."[78]

There have been times, however, when Lindsey has found it difficult to take advice from her husband, especially when he has something critical to say. "At first, I didn't like it," she says of the occasions that Thomas delivers a harsh truth about her performance. "I'd plead: 'Vonn, stop it. Be nice to me.'"[79] But as time wore on, both Vonns have come to understand that Thomas's critiques are not personal and that they do Lindsey a service by making her the best skier she can possibly be.

Although skiing is at the heart of both of their lives, the Vonns discuss a variety of topics as they travel around Europe and the United States. "As husband and wife we know that sometimes we have to flip the switch and be a normal couple, not a coach and athlete," says Lindsey. "We don't talk about racing as much as you might think."[80]

The Inner Circle of the "Vonntourage"

When she is not spending time with her husband, Lindsey Vonn maintains close relationships with other family members, particularly her brothers and sisters. As a group, Lindsey's four younger siblings endlessly support her. Their task is to help keep her calm and relaxed, especially before big events. Just prior to her big race at the 2010 Olympics, for example, they got together to bake, hang out, and let her shave her then eighteen-year-old brother

Reed's head. They thought it would help their sister get her mind off the task at hand if she could relax and do something silly. Her siblings are there for the more glamorous moments, too: Karin has accompanied Lindsey to several celebrity events, such as the 2011 MTV Movie Awards, and reportedly enjoys sharing in all the free products, gifts, and other perks frequently showered upon her sister by corporate sponsors.

Most importantly, the siblings are close, and none resent Lindsey for her fame and fortune. "She's just our big sister. We're proud more than anything," says Karin. "I've never felt jealous of her."[81] Vonn reciprocates that pride: When Karin graduated from the University of San Diego in May 2011, her older sister posted photos of her on Facebook and tweeted, "My sister Karin officially graduated from college today! So proud!! xo LV."[82]

Vonn also remains close with her mother, Linda Krohn, who remarried after her 2003 divorce from Vonn's father. Krohn has since moved to the Minneapolis suburb of Apple Valley. Krohn has supported her daughter's career and personal choices, and in particular has liked Thomas Vonn ever since he entered her daughter's life. "[Thomas] is so good to her, so that she only has to worry about ski racing," Krohn said. "It's a wonderful

Vonn pauses on the slopes to sign autographs for fans at the U.S. Alpine Championships at Sugarloaf in Carrabassett Valley, Maine, in March 2008.

Fluent in the Language of Skiing

Unlike many athletes, Lindsey Vonn is bilingual: She speaks English and German fluently. She took formal lessons in German and practiced by reading German children's books, which helped her increase her vocabulary. That she speaks German fluently is unusual for an American, but in her

Vonn's ability to speak fluent German is an asset when answering questions from the international media.

sport, it is an asset. German is sometimes called the language of skiing because it is spoken in many European skiing hot spots located in Switzerland, Germany, and Austria.

Knowing the language helps Vonn communicate with fans and reporters. During press conferences abroad she is often asked to reply to questions in German and does so skillfully and without complaint. Several of Vonn's trainers are Austrian, so knowing the language makes it easier to communicate with them, too. "The language of skiing is German, and I want to be a part of it," she said in 2007. "I'm in the sport for a long time, so I might as well be able to communicate." Vonn speaks German with an Austrian accent, which would be the equivalent of a person speaking English with a British or Australian accent.

Quoted in Nathaniel Vinton. "Skiing: Crash Can't Keep American Down." *New York Times*, January 29, 2007. www.nytimes.com/2007/01/29/sports/29iht-ski.4385022.html.

relationship."[83] Krohn reportedly hardly ever misses her daughter's races, even though she usually watches them on television or on the Internet. After each race Krohn typically sends an e-mail to Vonn letting her know how proud she is of her.

Vonn is not just warm and friendly to her family members. Although she is famous on the slopes for her bald aggression and crash-and-burn style, when the skis come off she is known as an approachable, friendly, girl-next-door type. Vonn is reportedly patient with fans, gracious and outgoing. She has been hailed as an all-American girl who just happens to be famous for an incredible talent. "She deserves every drop of success she finds … not just because she's an amazing skier but also because she's a stand-up human being," says *Ski Racing* magazine's Shauna Farnell. "Many racers who reach Vonn's star status would let it go to their heads, but not Lindsey. … She really couldn't be warmer or more approachable."[84]

"You Have to Accept It"

Despite her warmth and friendliness, Vonn remains estranged from her father, Alan Kildow. In the years after his daughter married Thomas Vonn, Kildow claimed to have come to terms with the fact that she married a man nine years her senior. "I was concerned over the fact that a teenage girl was dating a man nine years older than she was," he said in 2010. "But as time goes on, you have to accept it. When one's daughter chooses a husband, you need to accept him into the family, and we have."[85]

These feelings do not seem mutual, however. Kildow has reportedly left his daughter phone messages and e-mail notes, which she declines to return. Kildow did not attend the 2010 Olympic Games in Vancouver, thinking his presence might negatively affect his daughter's performance. Both parties refrain from speaking too much about the rift in public, stating only that the relationship is what it is and that it is not anybody's business but theirs.

It is no doubt immensely difficult, however, for Kildow to contend with the fact that the little girl he first introduced to the world of skiing has transformed into an international sensation—and he is not welcome in any part of her success. "Alan is suffering with it," says Erich Sailer, Lindsey's first coach from Buck Hill. Sailer predicts that the feud will not last forever, though. When Vonn is ready to have a family of her own and comes face-to-face with the difficulties of child rearing and the importance of family, Sailer predicts she will find a place once more for her father in her life. "Someday, after she goes through her racing career, she will have children," says Sailer. "It will be like another life. And he'll come back into her life."[86]

Promoting the Sport

Until that time, Vonn will keep herself busy with other pursuits. Among these are promoting the sport of skiing to the American people, who typically tend to follow skiing just every four years when a Winter Olympics rolls around. Vonn has become somewhat of an ambassador for the sport in her own country, and her goal is to raise Americans' interest in competitive skiing to the same level it enjoys in Europe.

Vonn respects that Americans can be fanatical about their sports, and she admits that skiing will likely never be as popular in the United States as baseball, football, and basketball. But she believes she can increase awareness of the sport on a competitive level and grow participation as well. "Ski racing is an amazing sport, and if more people knew about it, we would have more people following

Weird Interview Session

After Vonn had emerged as a World Cup champion, she joined about thirty local children in Vail, Colorado, for what was billed as "Epic Kids—Live with Lindsey." The televised event allowed her young fans to ask her probing questions. One of the most unusual queries Vonn received was whether she ever sneezed while racing downhill. She answered that she had not. "I don't breathe very much when I'm skiing," she said.

Quoted in Lauren Glendenning. "Vonn Takes Questions from Vail Kids," *Vail Daily News*, November 20, 2009. www.vaildaily.com/article/20091121/NEWS/911209948/1078&ParentProfile=1062.

it and more people doing it; not just ski racing, but skiing in general," she said. "I do think it's a part of my job as an athlete in the sport to try to promote ski racing as much as possible."[87]

Her Charitable Side

Vonn believes the success, fame, and fortune she has enjoyed comes with a responsibility to help those less fortunate than herself. She therefore gives both her time and money to charitable endeavors, including the Race to Erase MS, which seeks to eradicate multiple sclerosis, and the SOS Outreach program, which works to improve the lives of youth through outdoor adventure.

In 2009 she participated in an SOS Outreach question-and-answer session with Vail children. She urged the youngsters to explore the benefits of participation in outdoor activities. In May 2010 Vonn was a presenter at the Race to Erase MS Gala, which was held in Los Angeles. The affair raised a hefty sum of money to fight against and research the disease. That thrilled Vonn, who trumpeted the achievement on her Facebook page. "I have some great news, because of everyone's generosity we were able to raise 2 million dollars at the Race to Erase MS event!" she wrote. "I hope this will help to get us closer to a cure!"[88]

Vonn is particularly interested in promoting skiing among children, with whom she says she feels a special bond. She also feels an obligation to bring a spark to their lives. Part of this is due to her own influential childhood meeting with skiing star Picabo Street in 1995, which motivated her to maximize her own talents.

Though Vonn now belongs to the world, she has not forgotten about the children in her home state of Minnesota. After winning her first overall World Cup championship, she returned home to make an appearance at the same Bloomington skate and ski shop in which she met Street. As Vonn sat at a table, signed autographs, and answered questions from young skiers, she could not help but think back to that day thirteen years earlier. She hoped that she could make the same impact on a child that Street made on her. Vonn recalls, "I could see myself in every little girl that came up. I couldn't believe I was in the same position Picabo was when I met her, when I was the little girl who was so excited. When I met Picabo, it made me realize I could be a ski racer. It is so cool and so humbling to know I can be a role model now. It's just amazing to me that I'm in this place."[89] Street says of Vonn, "They couldn't ask for a better role model. She's tall and beautiful and strong and powerful and humble."[90]

Vonn arrives at the 2010 Race to Erase MS Gala event in Los Angeles, California, where she served as a presenter.

From the Course to the Courts

When she is not spending time with family, training for the slopes, or promoting skiing to America's youth, Lindsey Vonn enjoys other physical activities. She likes to play golf and bike ride, but her favorite sport—aside from skiing—is tennis. "I love to play tennis," she says. "It's something I enjoy doing in the summer."[91] Thomas excelled in tennis in high school and shared his passion with her before they were married. Lindsey reports that her backhand is good, but her forehand needs work and her volleys "are terrible."[92]

Vonn discovered that the athleticism and mobility required to compete at a moderately high level proved helpful to her on the slopes. "Tennis is really good for my agility and my hand-eye coordination," she told Tennis.com. "Tennis is a good way for me to stay light and quick on my feet, and be able to move my body well. It's really good cross-training for me."[93] Like any fan of any sport, she admires several professional players, including Andre Agassi and Andy Roddick. She once got to play a game with tennis legend Martina Navratilova, "but

Dream Role

Vonn is a television buff. Her favorite drama is *Law and Order*. So in 2010 when she received an opportunity to make a cameo appearance on the show, she jumped at it.

In the final episode of the 2010 season, Vonn had a small speaking part as a teacher's assistant who helps detectives find a man planning to blow up a school. Vonn was thrilled, but her joy was tempered when she learned that the episode on which she appeared would be the show's last: *Law and Order* was cancelled shortly thereafter. Vonn was shaken up over that news. "I don't know what I'd do [without it]," she said. "I have it [taped] and I watch it before I go to bed or work out."

http://articles.nydailynews.com/2010-05-17/entertainment/27064550_1_lindsey-vonn-olympics-skiing.

it was my first time playing on grass [courts], and I was not used to it, so I'm sure she thinks I'm terrible,"[94] Vonn said.

Most of all Vonn admires Swiss tennis star Roger Federer, who is arguably the finest player in the history of the sport. While training in Austria in June 2009, Vonn traveled to nearby Paris to watch Federer compete in the French Open. She told the Ski Channel that if she could ride a ski lift with anyone, it would be Federer.

The Other Side of Lindsey

The hectic schedule both on and off the slopes has sometimes made Vonn yearn for more serene activities. When calmer moods strike, she loves to read or watch her favorite TV show, *Law & Order*. She has also developed a passion for cooking and baking. "Lindsey's favorite place, besides the ski slope, is in the kitchen,"

Vonn poses with actor Jeremy Sisto on the set of the television series Law & Order *while filming a guest appearance on the show in April 2010.*

reports Snow.com dispatcher Sara Turner, who had the opportunity to cook with the skier in 2009. "She loves trying new recipes, baking healthy treats, and cooking for her friends and family."[95] Vonn shared with Turner a prized banana bread recipe that is healthy and low fat. "Lindsey's got this amazing banana bread recipe," testifies her mother. "It's so moist. So delicious."[96]

Among Vonn's main dish specialties are chicken schnitzel and pasta with tomato sauce and chicken. For dessert she sometimes likes to whip up sweets like pumpkin chocolate chip cookies. Even when she is not the chef, Vonn loves to eat. She enjoys chocolate, pizza, and anything with meat, and she has a particular weakness for kaiserschmaren, an Austrian pancake-like dessert made with raisins and powdered sugar.

Vonn claims her off-slope time is spent like most other Americans: with friends, indulging in relaxing activities. She reports that she and her friends like to watch movies or catch up over a cup of coffee. "Sometimes I'll make dinner at my house, or we'll all go over to my friend's house and watch TV. Other times, we'll go to a salon and get pedicures," she says. "It's just really fun stuff that we do together because we are not often together."[97]

Vonn is also a music lover, which is not surprising when one realizes that music helps propel her through the hours of workouts that are part of her intense training. Vonn likes pop, rap, and dance tunes—pretty much any music that has a beat to which she can work out. Among her favorites is pop star Justin Timberlake. "I'm a huge Justin fan!" she said in a 2010 interview posted on Timberlake's website. "I listen to his music when I work out all the time." Vonn also loves Beyoncé, T.I., Lil' Wayne, Lady Gaga, Dave Guetta, Kid Cudi, and Kanye West, but claims Timberlake is her favorite. As she told the singer's staff, "If you ever need a ski lesson you know who to call!"[98] Thomas Vonn claims his wife is easily starstruck, even as she was becoming quite the star herself.

Chapter 6

Not Just a Skier Anymore

The transformation from notable athlete to superstar is difficult for some sports figures. Some lose sight of their priorities, goals, and family. Others succumb to drug use or blow their money on flashy cars and houses. Lindsey Vonn, on the other hand, has handled the transition with ease. Her girl-next-door image remained intact after her 2010 Olympic gold-medal run thrust her into superstar status. She has enjoyed the media and fan attention in the United States but has kept her ego in check.

Vonn has kept busy with new endorsement deals, prominent media appearances, and glitzy social events. She has even been the subject of controversy. Both the positive and negative buzz surrounding the post-Olympic Vonn served to show how she had become a prominent, news-making athlete, one that is both scrutinized and admired.

Shining with the Stars

Vonn was honored in many different ways after earning Olympic gold. For example, she was delighted to be a guest at the 2010 White House Correspondents' dinner. This annual event is hosted by an organization of journalists who cover the White House and the president. President Barack Obama spoke at the May affair that the Vonns attended.

Vonn speaks with an interviewer from Access Hollywood *after attending the 2010 White House Correspondents' Dinner.*

Despite the prestige of being invited to such an event, Vonn had a hard time accepting her star status. She felt embarrassed and out of place when she found herself in the company of award-winning actors and famous musicians. Although Vonn did not meet Obama at the function, she mingled with celebrities such as Russell Crowe, Julia Roberts, and Alec Baldwin, as well as rock-and-roll icon Jon Bon Jovi. It was a bit overwhelming for her. "For the life of me, I could not figure out what I was doing there,"[99] she said. She caught the eye of husband Thomas and gave him a knowing look. "We laughed," he said, "because we were thinking the same thing: 'These are not the people we were having dinner with a year ago.'"[100]

Vonn was also honored by *Glamour* magazine, which in 2010 presented her with one of its Women of the Year Awards. "For women today, there are no limits," Vonn said. "We play hard, get down and dirty, and kick butt. And we're going to set new and higher standards for the female athletes of the future."[101] *Glamour* placed Vonn in elite company. Among the other women honored were Queen Rania of Jordan, pop star Fergie, and Dr. Hawa Abdi of Somalia, who has treated thousands of poor women and children free of charge. Vonn expressed surprise that she was so

An Inside Look at Lindsey

The 2010 Olympic gold won by Lindsey Vonn created interest in how she was able to perform at such a high level. That is why high-definition television network Epix aired a documentary titled *Lindsey Vonn: In the Moment* in March 2011.

The show was a well-rounded look at Vonn. It included videos of her in competition, as well as in training and handling the media spotlight. The program also featured interviews with Vonn that revealed her inner thoughts about herself and her sport. She spoke about how competitive skiing molded her and taught her more about her capabilities as a person and what motivates her.

"I think this sport teaches you a lot about yourself and what type of person you are inside," she said in the documentary. "I think I've dug deep within myself to figure out what it is that I want, what it is that I dream of doing, what it is that I want to become, what truly defined me."

Quoted in Epix. *Lindsey Vonn: In The Moment*. March 2011. www.epixhd.com/lindsey-vonn-in-the-moment.

---

honored. "I just couldn't believe it," she said. "Something like this doesn't normally happen to a skier like me."[102]

Talk Show Circuit

But Vonn herself was a sought-after celebrity after the Olympics. She served as a guest speaker at a number of events, many of which were hosted by local organizations. She also landed spots as a presenter in such prestigious television events as the Academy of Country Music Awards and the ESPYs, the annual awards show hosted by the cable sports network ESPN.

Vonn was invited to appear on several of the most iconic television talk shows in America as well. The most notable of these was *The Tonight Show with Jay Leno*, which was aired just a week after the Olympics ended. Vonn brought her gold medal to the set and was greeted by chants of "USA! USA! USA!"[103] from the audience. There was no hint of bragging about her accomplishments throughout the interview, though. Vonn came off as natural, humble, and funny. When asked by Leno about the pinkie she broke during the giant slalom event, for example, she said she was supposed to tape the finger to the one next to it, but did not because the tape "did not really match my dress."[104]

Vonn was also a guest on *The Ellen DeGeneres Show*, *Access Hollywood*, *The Daily 10*, and *The Tonight Show* when it was hosted by Conan O'Brien. She also joined interviewer Michael Kay on a New York City talk show titled *CenterStage* and was a guest on the radio program *On Air with Ryan Seacrest*, which features the host of the iconic reality show *American Idol*.

Lindsey Goes Commercial

Like many athletes, Vonn has several corporate sponsors that pay her to advertise their products. Her endorsement contracts add up to thousands of dollars of income every year. Vonn's corporate sponsors include Red Bull, Under Armour, Audi, and Alka-Seltzer.

Some corporate sponsors did not even wait until Vonn won gold in the 2010 Olympics to sign her up. International Marketing Group agent Sue Dorf, who handles Vonn, explained before the Olympics began that Vonn was a fresh face who could capture the imagination of the American consumer. "The general public has a thirst for something new and I think Lindsey is going to quench that," she said. "To the vast majority of Americans, she will be new. She is going to be a very intriguing story, in light of her accomplishments, in light of how beautiful she is."[105] *USA Today* writer David Leon Moore explained that Vonn's appeal stemmed from her identity as a "wholesome, articulate and athletically gifted woman."[106]

In an era in which beauty was personified by skinny supermodels, Vonn indeed represented a new breed of attractive women. She was 175 pounds (79.4kg) but curvy and without a trace of fat. Her prettiness and athleticism motivated Under Armour to

Vonn sports clothing and a water bottle with the logos of Red Bull and Under Armor, two of the many companies with which she has signed sponsorship deals.

feature her in a commercial in which she was shown in the midst of an intense workout wearing their workout apparel.

Another company that embraced Vonn was Proctor & Gamble, which relied on her attractive features to sell beauty products such as shampoo, makeup, and soap. And just as Proctor & Gamble embraced her, she in turn embraced the notion of peddling such items. "I love getting glammed up," she said. "I think all women enjoy getting dolled up."[107]

Michael Kay Trivia Questions

Most interviewers in the American media focus on Vonn's achievements, particularly in the 2010 Olympics. There was one exception: Michael Kay, who hosts a talk show called *CenterStage* for New York City audiences.

Vonn was a guest on that program in June 2010. Kay asked her a number of questions about her likes and dislikes during a segment he dubbed "Hit and Run." Among the tidbits of information she revealed to Kay was that her favorite book is *The Great Gatsby*, her favorite movie is *Gladiator*, and her favorite late-night snack is chocolate vanilla fudge ice cream. She also revealed she is afraid of insects.

Kay also asked Vonn about her visualization technique before a race. Vonn answered that she does indeed visualize what she needs to do throughout the run. "You visualize every bump, every turn," she said. She then explained that the visualization process begins after her initial experience with a slope in a training run. "After the first [downhill] run, I'll visualize it maybe 100 times," she said.

Lindsey Vonn. *CenterStage*. YES, June 2010.

Photo Controversy

In addition to appearing on product packaging, Vonn has been the subject of many magazine covers and photo shoots. In addition to being famous and newsworthy, Vonn is also very pretty, and thus makes for an excellent photo subject.

Some photo shoots, however, have generated controversy. The 2010 *Sports Illustrated* cover featuring Vonn caused a particular stir. The photo displayed her bent forward on a hill in a skiing outfit and smiling for the camera. Despite the fact that she was fully clothed and in a sports-related position, some thought the way she was positioned was degrading to women. Others complained that the position inappropriately sexualized her. According to Nicole M. LaVoi, associate director of the Tucker Center for Research on Girls & Women in Sport at the University of Minnesota, over a sixty-year period, only about 4 percent of all *Sports Illustrated* covers have featured women—and the vast majority of these have appeared in either skimpy outfits such as bikinis or in sexualized positions. "When females are featured on the cover of *SI*, they are more likely than not to be in sexualized poses and not in action," wrote LaVoi on her blog. "The most recent Vonn cover is no exception."[108]

Many others strongly disagreed, however. "Call me a 21st century male chauvinist pig," wrote *Denver Post* sports columnist Patrick Saunder, "but I don't find anything degrading about the cover."[109] Ashley Furrow, writing on the website Bleacher Report, agreed. "Why can't she be both the best skier in the world and really, really attractive too, as the cover portrays her?"[110] Vonn agreed with these sentiments, pointing out that the tuck pose in which she was photographed is the exact position in which she skis. "I think it was just blown out of proportion," she said. "There's nothing sexual or controversial about it. ... I actually thought it was a cool picture and great for my sport."[111]

Various other photos of the ski star have caused even more controversy, especially those that show her in sexy, skimpy outfits, including bikinis. One Olympic edition of *Sports Illustrated* featured a multipage spread in which Vonn was clad in a bikini. She was shown with various backgrounds, including in a chalet and a sauna and on a glacier. Those pictures met with criticism as well. Ultimately, though, most people chalked up the controversy to the fact that Vonn happens to be a very attractive person as well as a first-class athlete. As sportswriter Chris Chase put it, "Vonn isn't a good looking athlete, she's a great athlete who happens to be good looking."[112]

Back to Work

Vonn did not bask for too long in post-Olympic attention or controversy, however. After the Games and the conclusion of the 2009–2010 World Cup season, she continued an intense training schedule. Though she dominated the downhill and super

G in World Cup competition during the 2009–2010 season, she ranked only fourteenth in the world in the slalom and a disappointing twenty-eighth in the giant slalom. Soon she was back on the slopes for the 2010–2011 season, where her three-year hold on the championship ended in controversy.

Vonn peaked in France in mid-December 2010. She earned gold in the downhill, super combined, and super G. During that month and in January 2011, she won medals in eleven of fourteen events. After a mediocre showing at the World Ski Championships in Germany, she recovered by late February to make another brilliant run, winning four golds, three silvers, and one bronze during an eight-race stretch in Sweden, Italy, and Czechoslovakia.

She had a chance to snag her fourth consecutive World Cup crown heading into the last day of the final event in Switzerland. She sat 3 points behind archrival Maria Riesch when the giant slalom was called off due to bad weather. World Cup races are not made up, however, so Vonn did not even get the chance to attempt the race. It meant her shot at winning the title was lost. She was too upset to speak with the media, but her message through the U.S. Ski Team echoed her frustration. "Win or lose I just wanted the chance," she said. "I feel devastated."[113] Vonn added her belief that the rules should be changed so that races postponed during the final week of the season are rescheduled.

Vonn races in the super G event at the Alpine World Skiing Championships in Garmisch-Partenkirchen, Germany, in February 2011.

Amazing Comeback

Although Vonn fell short of capturing a fourth straight World Cup championship, she certainly made a late run at it. She was a whopping 216 points behind Maria Riesch a mere month before the end of the season.

Vonn lost nearly the entire month of February to a concussion sustained in Germany during a practice run for the giant slalom. Her return to the slopes signaled the beginning of her furious charge to the top. It started in early March in Tarvisio, Italy. Vonn was at her scintillating best, taking gold medals in the combined disciplines and super G and adding a pair of silver

Vonn kisses the trophy she was awarded for her victory in the super G at the World Cup finals in Switzerland in March 2011. Despite her success, she was not able to overtake Germany's Maria Riesch for the overall championship.

medals. The Tarvisio event alone chopped her deficit to just 96 points and brought Vonn confidence. But she also understood an uphill climb remained. "I'm going to still keep fighting until the very last race," she said. "I feel fresh still. I feel like I have a lot of energy, and this is where you have to kick in the sixth gear."[114]

Her first medal performance ever in the giant slalom the following week in Czechoslovakia helped her overtake Riesch and launch herself into first place in the overall standings. But Riesch wrested the lead away in Switzerland and clinched the title when the final race—the giant slalom—was canceled.

Despite losing the distinction as defending World Cup champion, Vonn led her fellow skiers with eight gold medals. That earned her $510,000 for the year, which edged out the total winnings for Riesch. And she felt a sense of pride about giving Riesch a scare at the end of the season. "I'm extremely proud to have been in the fight," Vonn said. "A few weeks ago I was over 200 points behind."[115]

Branching Out

Vonn looks ahead to the 2011–2012 World Cup season and, ultimately, the 2014 Winter Olympics, which will be held in Sochi, Russia. Some speculated that Vonn would not participate, but she quickly dispelled those rumors. She even left open the possibility of competing in the 2018 Games, particularly if they are held in Denver, Colorado.

Fans of Vonn can expect her to attempt to thrive in events that have previously not been her strength. Although she is proud of what she has accomplished in downhill competitions, Vonn is no longer satisfied to dominate just speed events. She yearns to win medals in technical disciplines, such as the slalom and giant slalom. Of her thirty-three World Cup titles heading into the 2011 season, she had won just two in the slalom. She was quick to admit that she needed to improve, saying, "I've always struggled with those two events."[116] She committed to competing in the 2014 Games, knowing that people will expect her to win more medals than she did in 2010. After all, she had only

Vonn smiles after completing her run in the giant slalom event at a World Cup event in the Czech Republic in March 2011. After achieving great success as a downhill racer, she hopes to continue to improve her skill in the technical events, including slalom and giant slalom.

captured one gold medal in Vancouver. The pressure is on to prove she is a versatile a skier who can win multiple medals in multiple disciplines.

To this end, in 2010 she began to adjust her training schedule to focus more on the skills required for the technical events. She isolated herself in an Austrian gym and worked out a grueling eight hours a day. She also moved outdoors to work on her explosiveness, quickness, and agility. She knew she had to become more athletic to win events that were not based solely on speed and power skiing. "I still lifted weights inside and rode a billion miles on a bike in the gym," she said. "But I added drills to improve my foot speed. I'd say half my time was outside working on my footwork and getting my feet quicker. It worked."[117] She has also altered her diet to get in better shape. She has eliminated rice, pasta, bread, and dairy products, for example.

These changes worked well enough early in the 2010–2011 season when she competed in a slalom race in Finland. An off-balance turn early in the competition nearly sent her sprawling into the snow. But she made a remarkable recovery and finished a respectable sixth. She knew that her new workout regimen had saved her in that event. She also placed among the top ten in the giant slalom several times, including World Cup races in Czechoslovakia and Switzerland in December. She peaked with a bronze medal performance in Czechoslovakia in March 2011.

Only time would tell if those small triumphs would translate into huge wins in the future. But she had already won more World Cup medals than any skier in American history, and Vonn was hopeful that her winning streak would continue and that she would ultimately triumph in the 2014 Olympics. "You don't want to look too far ahead," she said, "but, yeah, I want to go back and win again at the Olympics."[118]

Family in the Future?

That competition and her desire to improve on the gold-medal performance in the 2010 Games had Vonn giving little thought to much else in her life. But after four years of marriage, she was sometimes asked about whether she had any dreams to start a family while maintaining her skiing career. Her answer was invariably that she did not feel it would be a good mix. Whatever Vonn does, she seeks to do it to the best of her ability. She doubted that she could maximize her potential as a world-class skier while raising kids. Nor did she believe she could do her best job as a mother while maintaining her skiing career. "I want to keep skiing as long as I can," she said. "I want to stay 100 percent focused on my skiing. And then when I'm done, I want to be 100 percent focused on my family. I don't want to mix the two."[119]

It was no wonder she did not want anything to hinder her skiing. She was already the greatest skier her nation had ever produced.

Introduction: Lindsey Vonn: American Phenomenon

1. Quoted in Amy Van Deusen. "Lindsey Vonn." *Women's Health*, February 2010. www.womenshealthmag.com/fitness/lindsey-vonn-3.
2. Alan Abrahamson. "Lindsey Vonn: Designed to Win." NBC Olympics, January 11, 2010. http://i.nbcolympics.com/news-features/news/newsid=389228.html.

Chapter 1: From Turtle to Hare

3. Quoted in Bill Pennington. "Lindsey Vonn at the Summit." *New York Times Magazine*, February 3, 2010. www.nytimes.com/2010/02/07/magazine/07Vonn-t.html.
4. Quoted in Jim Souhan. "It's Full Speed Ahead for Lindsey Kildow." *Minneapolis StarTribune*, March 14, 2008. www.startribune.com/sports/16689326.html.
5. Quoted in Meri-Jo Borzilleri. "Fearless Style Has Vonn on Verge of Skiing History." ESPN.com, March 11, 2008. http://sports.espn.com/oly/skiing/news/story?id=3286757.
6. Quoted in David Leon Moore. "Skier Lindsey Vonn Following Idol to the Mountaintop." *USA Today*, February 21, 2008. www.usatoday.com/sports/olympics/2008-02-20-vonn-1c-cover_N.htm.
7. Quoted in Dave Perry. "Ski Champ Has a 'Lot of Moxie.'" *Explorer*, February 24, 2010. http://explorernews.com/news/pima_pinal/article_0fff76ac-a165-55f5-9e8b-f4960cb25ca6.html.
8. Quoted in Pennington. "Lindsey Vonn at the Summit."
9. Quoted in Barry Svrluga. "From Turtle to Snow Hare: Kildow Is Learning to Harness Speed." *Washington Post*, December 9, 2005. http://www.washingtonpost.com/wp-dyn/content/article/2005/12/08/AR2005120802039.html
10. Quoted in Pennington. "Lindsey Vonn at the Summit."
11. Quoted in Pennington. "Lindsey Vonn at the Summit."

12. Quoted in Murphy. "Smashing Success." *Sports Illustrated*, March 10, 2008. http://sportsillustrated.cnn.com/vault/article/magazine/MAG1109942/index.htm.

13. Quoted in Pennington. "Lindsey Vonn at the Summit."

14. Quoted in Rachel Blount. "Lindsey Vonn: On Top of the World." *Minneapolis StarTribune*, December 25, 2008. www.startribune.com/templates/Print_This_Story?sid=36708369.

15. Quoted in Afin.com. "Lindsey Vonn: Sport-Star." www.afin.at/243.0.html.

16. Quoted in Tim Layden. "Ready to Rock." *Sports Illustrated*, February 18, 2010. http://sportsillustrated.cnn.com/vault/article/magazine/MAG1165550/index.htm.

17. Quoted in Pennington. "Lindsey Vonn at the Summit."

Chapter 2: Bumps on the Road to Stardom

18. Quoted in Paula Parrish. "Kildow Wins Super Series Super-G." *Rocky Mountain News*, November 27, 2000, Sports p. 29C.

19. Quoted in John Meyer. "Steamboat's Lalive Gives Way to Vail Teen." *Denver Post*, February 15, 2002.

20. Quoted in Parrish. "Kildow Wins Super Series Super-G," Sports p. 29C.

21. Quoted in Jay Weiner. "Beyond Buck Hill; For Lindsey Kildow, Who Trained in Burnsville and Is One of the U.S. Ski Team's 'Buck Hill Four,' Becoming an Olympian Was All a Part of the Master Plan." *Minneapolis StarTribune*, February 20, 2002, p. 01A.

22. Quoted in Philip Hersh. "She's Picking up Speed." *Chicago Tribune*, January 28, 2005. http://articles.chicagotribune.com/2005-01-28/sports/0501280304_1_lindsey-kildow-picabo-street-ski-school.

23. Quoted in Meyer. "Steamboat's Lalive Gives Way to Vail Teen."

24. Quoted in Meyer. "Steamboat's Lalive Gives Way to Vail Teen."

25. Quoted in Meyer. "Steamboat's Lalive Gives Way to Vail Teen."

26. Quoted in John Meyer. "U.S. Believes Better Olympics Ahead; Vail Teen Kildow Considered Key Component." *Denver Post*, February 25, 2002.

27. Quoted in Meyer. "U.S. Believes Better Olympics Ahead; Vail Teen Kildow Considered Key Component."

28. Quoted in Layden. "Ready to Rock."
29. Quoted in Charles Robinson. "Frenemy Lines: Vonn Seals Spot as USA's 'Top Dog.'" Yahoo! Sports, February 17, 2011. http://sports.yahoo.com/olympics/vancouver/alpine_skiing/news?slug=cr-vonnmancuso021709.
30. Quoted in Layden. "Ready to Rock."
31. Pennington. "Lindsey Vonn at the Summit."
32. Quoted in Pennington. "Lindsey Vonn at the Summit."
33. Quoted in Murphy. "Smashing Success."
34. Quoted in Murphy. "Smashing Success."

Chapter 3: Falling, Recovering, Winning

35. Quoted in John Meyer. "Kildow's Promise Multiplies." *Denver Post*, February 25, 2004, p. D.
36. Quoted in Pat Graham. "Vancouver Olympics: Lindsey Vonn's Strained Relationship with Father." *Huffington Post Denver*, February 9, 2010. www.huffingtonpost.com/2010/02/09/vancouver-olympics-lindsa_n_455688.html.
37. Quoted in Pennington. "Lindsey Vonn at the Summit."
38. Quoted in Ski Racing. "USST's Daron Rahlves and Lindsey Kildow Win National Championship Super G." www.skiracing.com/?q=node/2088.
39. Quoted in Meyer. "Kildow's Promise Multiplies," p. D.
40. Quoted in Meyer. "Kildow's Promise Multiplies," p. D.
41. Quoted in Matt Youson. "Lindsey Vonn, Snow Queen." *Independent*, February 3, 2009. www.independent.co.uk/life-styke/redbulletin/lindsey-vonn-snow-queen-1657685.html.
42. Quoted in Erica Bulman. "Kildow Crashes During Training at Worlds." *USA Today*, January 31, 2005. www.usatoday.com/sports/olympics/winter/2005-01-31-roundup_x.htm.
43. Quoted in Tim Layden. "Kildow Feels Heat of the Spotlight." *Sports Illustrated*, February 7, 2005. http://sportsillustrated.cnn.com/vault/article/magazine/MAG1108490/index.htm.
44. Quoted in Graham. "Vancouver Olympics."
45. Quoted in Pennington. "Lindsey Vonn at the Summit."

46. Quoted in Kevin Johnson and Andy Gardiner. "Kildow Not Giving Up Hope of Racing After Crash." *USA Today*, February 13, 2006. www.usatoday.com/sports/olympics/torino/alpine/2006-02-13-womens-downhill_x.htm.

47. Quoted in Bob Baum, Associated Press. "Kildow Takes Scary Fall but Still Hopes to Compete." Fredericksburg.com, February 14, 2006. www.fredericksburg.com/News/FLS/2006/022006/02142006/167960/index_html?page=1.

48. Quoted in Clay Latimer. "Kildow Still Dreams Big." *Rocky Mountain News*, November 18, 2006. http://m.rockymountainnews.com/news/2006/Nov/18/kildow-still-dreams-big.

49. Quoted in Andreas Hipfl. "New Era for Lindsey." Red Bull, September 10, 2009. www.redbullusa.com/cs/Satellite/en_US/Article/New-Era-for-Lindsey-021242780072905.

Chapter 4: Grabbing the Gold

50. Quoted in Layden. "Ready to Rock."

51. Quoted in Layden. "Ready to Rock."

52. Quoted in Juliann Fritz. "World Cup Ski: Lindsey Kildow Takes Silver in Worlds DH." *Outdoor News Wire*, February 12, 2007. http://www.skibumnews.com/racing.htm.

53. Quoted in Mark Sappenfield. "U.S. Skiers Miller and Vonn Win Overall World Cup." *Christian Science Monitor*, March 17, 2008. www.csmonitor.com/World/Europe/2008/0317/p01s01-woeu.html.

54. Quoted in CNN. "Vonn Wins 2nd Gold at World Ski Championships." February 9, 2009. http://edition.cnn.com/2009/SPORT/02/09/skiing.women/index.html.

55. Quoted in Nate Peterson. "Lindsey Vonn Makes It Back-to-Back Overall World Cup Titles." *New York Times*, March 11, 2009. www.nytimes.com/2009/03/12/sports/othersports/12ski.html.

56. Quoted in Layden. "Ready to Rock."

57. Quoted in Layden. "Ready to Rock."

58. Brian Gomez. "Vonn Overcomes Bruised Shin, Wins Olympic Downhill." *Colorado Springs Gazette*, February 17, 2010. www.gazette.com/articles/downhill-94322-early-leader.html.

59. Quoted in Associated Press. "Vonn, Mancuso Go 1-2 in Downhill." ESPN.com, February 17, 2010. http://m.espn.go.com/nhl/story?storyId=4921825&wjb.

60. Steve Daly. "Lindsey Vonn Wins Gold in Women's Downhill Ski Event." *People*, February 17, 2010. www.people.com/people/article/0,,20345163,00.html.

61. Gomez. "Vonn Overcomes Bruised Shin, Wins Olympic Downhill."

62. Ash Marshall. "Lindsey Vonn Wins Gold in Her Greatest Performance Ever." Bleacher Report, February 17, 2010. http://bleacherreport.com/articles/347345-2010-winter-olympics-lindsey-vonn-wins-gold-greatest-performance-ever.

63. Quoted in Bill Pennington. "Vonn Wins Olympic Gold in Downhill with Daring Run." *New York Times,* February 17, 2010. www.nytimes.com/2010/02/18/sports/olympics/18downhill.html?adxnnl=1&adxnnlx=1311883886-6LvIFj3go77DkK7bbd29BQ.

64. Quoted in Associated Press. "Vonn, Mancuso Go 1-2 in Downhill."

65. Pennington. "Von Wins Olympic Gold in Downhill with Daring Run."

66. Quoted in Howard Bryant. "Vonn Pushes Through Injury for Gold." ESPN.com, February 18, 2010. http://sports.espn.go.com/olympics/winter/2010/alpineskiing/columns/story?columnist=bryant_howard&id=4922928.

67. Ron Judd. "Lindsey Vonn Wins Gold in Downhill Despite All Obstacles." *Seattle Times*, February 17, 2010. http://seattletimes.nwsource.com/html/ronjudd/2011110720_judd118.html.

68. Mike Lopresti. "Golden Lindsey Vonn: 'This Is the Best Day of My Life.'" *USA Today*, February 17, 2010. www.usatoday.com/sports/columnist/lopresti/2010-02-17-lindsey-vonn_N.htm.

69. Quoted in Associated Press. "Vonn Wins Third Straight World Cup Title." ESPN.com. March 12, 2010. http://sports.espn.go.com/oly/skiing/news/story?id=4988519.

70. Quoted in Charlotte Massey. "Meet U.S. Skier Lindsey Vonn." *Time For Kids*, February 24, 2010. www.timeforkids. com/TFK/kids/news/story/0,28277,1967833,00.html.

71. Quoted in Lorenzo Benet. "Olympic Skier Lindsey Kildow Recalls Wedding Jitters." *People*, October 20, 2007. www. people.com/people/article/0,,20153317,00.html.

72. Quoted in Pennington. "Lindsey Vonn at the Summit."

73. Quoted in Benet. "Olympic Skier Lindsey Kildow Recalls Wedding Jitters."

74. Quoted in Min-Q Kim. "Exclusive Interview: Lindsey Vonn, America's Sweetheart Going for Gold." JustinTimberlake. com, February 5, 2010. www.justintimberlake.com/news/ exclusive_interview_lindsey_vonn_americas_sweetheart_ going_for_gold.

75. Quoted in Layden. "Ready to Rock."

76. Quoted in David Leon Moore. "Lindsey Vonn's Injury Tempers Huge Olympics Expectations." *USA Today*, February 12, 2010. www.usatoday.com/sports/olympics/vancouver/alpine/ 2010-02-11-lindsey-vonn-cover_N.htm.

77. Quoted in Hipfl. "New Era for Lindsey."

78. Quoted in Hipfl. "New Era for Lindsey."

79. Quoted in Pennington. "Lindsey Vonn at the Summit."

80. Quoted in Pennington. "Lindsey Vonn at the Summit."

81. Quoted in Kelley McMillan. "Vonn Bakes Banana Bread Before Today's Downhill." *Skiing*. www.skinet.com/skiing/ fondue-party/ski-culture/2010/02/vonn-bakes-banana- bread-before-todays-downhill.

82. Lindsey Vonn. Twitter. May 22, 2011. http://twitter.com/#!/ lindseyvonn/status/72377428516929536.

83. Quoted in Graham. "Vancouver Olympics."

84. Shauna Farnell. "Lindsey Vonn Is a Star but She's Nice, Too." *Ski Racing*, December 6, 2010. www.skiracing.com/ ?q=node/776.

85. Quoted in Pennington. "Lindsey Vonn at the Summit."

86. Quoted in Pennington. "Lindsey Vonn at the Summit."

87. Quoted in *Manila Bulletin*. "Lindsey Vonn Is 2010 AP Female Athlete of Year." December 19, 2010.

88. Quoted in Facebook. "Links on Lindsey Vonn." May 12, 2010. www.facebook.com/posted.php?id=89975379727&share_id=138680569475571&comments=1.

89. Quoted in Blount. "Lindsey Vonn."

90. Quoted in John Meyer. "Flying V: Here Comes Lindsey Vonn." *Denver Post*, February 12, 2010. www.denverpost.com/olympics/ci_14378234?source=pkg.

91. Quoted in Massey. "Meet U.S. Skier Lindsey Vonn."

92. Quoted in Sarah Thurmond. "Q&A with Lindsey Vonn, Olympic Skier and 'Federer Freak.'" Tennis.com, December 23, 2009. www.tennis.com/articles/templates/thespin.aspx?articleid=3032&zoneid=8.

93. Quoted in Thurmond. "Q&A with Lindsey Vonn, Olympic Skier and 'Federer Freak.'"

94. Quoted in Thurmond. "Q&A with Lindsey Vonn, Olympic Skier and 'Federer Freak.'"

95. Sara Turner. "Cooking with Lindsey Vonn: Banana Bread." Snow.com, February 4, 2010. http://buzz.snow.com/channels/mountain_channels/vail-mountain/b/dispatches/archive/2010/02/04/cooking-with-lindsey-vonn-banana-bread.aspx.

96. Quoted in Kelly Macmillan. "Lindsey Vonn Prepares for Winter Olympics Downhill Ski." *Skiing*, February 2010. www.skinet.com/skiing/fondue-party/ski-culture/2010/02/vonn-bakes-banana-bread-before-todays-downhill.

97. Quoted in Massey. "Meet U.S. Skier Lindsey Vonn."

98. Quoted in Kim. "Exclusive Interview."

Chapter 6: Not Just a Skier Anymore

99. Quoted in Bill Pennington. "From the Slopes to the Red Carpet." *New York Times*, December 1, 2010. www.nytimes.com/2010/12/02/sports/02vonn.html.

100. Quoted in Pennington. "From the Slopes to the Red Carpet."

101. Quoted in Shaun Dreisbach. "Lindsey Vonn, Mia Hamm & Lisa Leslie: The Game Changers." *Glamour*, November 1, 2010. www.glamour.com/women-of-the-year/2010/lindsey-vonn-mia-hamm-and-lisa-leslie.

102. Quoted in Epix. *Lindsey Vonn: In The Moment*. March 2011. www.epixhd.com/lindsey-vonn-in-the-moment.

103. Lindsey Vonn. *The Tonight Show with Jay Leno*. NBC, March 1, 2010.

104. Lindsey Vonn. *The Tonight Show with Jay Leno*.

105. Quoted in *SportsBusiness Daily*. "Lindsey Vonn Could Ride Momentum to Marketing Gold Next Year." March 13, 2009. www.sportsbusinessdaily.com/Daily/Issues/2009/03/Issue-122/Sponsorships-Advertising-Marketing/Lindsey-Vonn-Could-Ride-Momentum-To-Marketing-Gold-Next-Year. aspx.

106. David Leon Moore. "Glamour Aside, Vonn Focuses on Vancouver Gold." *USA Today*, September 30, 2009. www.usatoday.com/sports/olympics/2009-09-29-lindseyvonnad-campaign_N.htm.

107. Quoted in Moore. " Glamour Aside, Vonn Focuses on Vancouver Gold."

108. Nicole M. LaVoi. "Vonn Watch: *Sports Illustrated* Cover Is Predictable." *One Sport Voice*, February 2, 2010. www.womentalksports.com/items/read/38/162903.

109. Patrick Saunder. "Vonn's *SI* Cover: Sexist or Not?" *Denver Post*, February 5, 2010. www.denverpost.com/sports/ci_14341638#ixzz1TW816Eof.

110. Ashley Furrow. "Lindsey Vonn's Controversial *SI* Cover: People Need to Grow Up." Bleacher Report, February 5, 2010. http://bleacherreport.com/articles/340334-lindsey-vonns-controversial-si-cover-people-need-to-grow-up.

111. Quoted in *Time*. "10 Questions for Lindsey Vonn." March 8, 2010. www.time.com/time/magazine/article/0,9171,1968114,00.html.

112. Chris Chase. "Lindsey Vonn Poses for *Sports Illustrated*'s Swimsuit Issue." Yahoo! Sports, February 9, 2010. http://sports.yahoo.com/olympics/blog/fourth_place_medal/post/Lindsey-Vonn-poses-for-Sports-Illustrated-s-swim?urn=oly-218547.

113. Quoted in Brian Homewood. "Riesch Wins World Cup After Race Scrapped." WSAU.com, March 18, 2011. www.wsau.com/news/articles/2011/mar/18/riesch-wins-world-cup-after-race-scrapped.

114. Quoted in Karel Janicek. "Vonn, Riesch in Race for World Cup Overall Title." *Washington Post*, March 10, 2011. www.washingtonpost.com/wp-dyn/content/article/2011/03/10/AR2011031003001.html.

115. Quoted in Graham Dunbar. "Lindsey Vonn Feels 'Devastated' to Lose World Cup Title." Associated Press, March 19, 2011. www.signonsandiego.com/news/2011/mar/19/lindsey-vonn-devastated-to-lose-world-cup-title.

116. Quoted in Bonnie D. Ford. "Lindsey Vonn Looks to Add Versatility." ESPN.com, November 8, 2010. http://espn.go.com/blog/olympics/post/_/id/27/lindsey-vonn-looks-to-dominate-while-improving.

117. Quoted in Pennington. "From the Slopes to the Red Carpet."

118. Quoted in Pennington. "From the Slopes to the Red Carpet."

119. Quoted in Jeff Slonim. "Lindsey Vonn Puts Parenthood on the Back Burner." *People*, March 21, 2010. http://celebritybabies.people.com/2010/03/21/lindsey-vonn-puts-parenthood-on-the-back-burner.

1984

Born in Burnsville, Minnesota, on October 18.

1987

Starts skiing for first time around Buck Hill slopes.

1991

Begins taking skiing lessons from Erich Sailer.

1993–1994

Travels to Europe with Sailer to train.

1994

Lindsey meets Olympic skiing champion Picabo Street at a ski shop near her childhood home.

1997

Shows enough promise as a skier to motivate her parents to move family to Vail, Colorado.

1999

Wins slalom at the Trofeo Topolino event in Italy; places twice in the top six in International Ski Federation slalom events in Colorado; takes second place in successive slalom Nor-Am Cup races in Canada.

2000

Takes her first medal in FIS competition by earning silver; makes World Cup debut in Utah soon after her sixteenth birthday; wins her first gold medal in an FIS race with a victory in the giant slalom in Colorado in April; captures her first Super Series triumph with a win in the super G in Colorado in November; begins competing against other top-level youth skiers in Europa Cup events.

2002

Competes in Winter Olympics and outshines all other American female skiers; begins dating future husband, Thomas Vonn; mother files for divorce as Lindsey's relationship with her father begins to deteriorate; a crash in December in Canada knocks her out of competition for a month.

2003

Bike ride through mountains with fellow skier Julia Mancuso puts into focus the need to intensify training.

2004

Earns her first World Cup medal by placing third in a downhill race in Italy; takes her first World Cup gold with a downhill victory in Canada.

2005

An accident in February during a training run for the World Ski Championships hinders her performance; in December, becomes first American female skier since Picabo Street to win a World Cup event in successive years.

2006

Competes in 2006 Winter Games despite an injury from a crash during training; begins to thrive in World Cup competition for first time, taking several gold and silver medals early in the 2006-2007 season.

2007

Earns three gold and five other medals in World Cup competition; marries Thomas Vonn in Utah.

2008

Wins the overall and downhill World Cup championship.

2009

Hurts thumb on broken champagne bottle while celebrating gold-medal performance in World Ski Championships; captures two gold medals in World Cup event in Italy; captures several golds in super G and slalom during remarkable run in March; takes second consecutive World Cup crown; lands several endorsement deals from corporate sponsors.

2010

Grabs gold in 11 World Cup races to gain momentum leading up to the Winter Olympics; a shin injury sustained during a training run puts her Olympic performance in jeopardy; earns first Olympic gold medal in downhill event in Vancouver; wins eleven World Cup gold medals to take her third consecutive overall title; honored by *Glamour* magazine in its Women of the Year issue.

2011

Takes three gold medals and four silver medals during impressive eight-race stretch in World Cup competition; shows improvement in giant slalom with bronze-medal performance in Czechoslovakia in March; strong comeback against Maria Riesch falls short as Lindsey loses World Cup championship after winning three straight.

For More Information

Books

Kylie Burns. *Alpine and Freestyle Skiing*. New York: Crabtree, 2009. This book features stories, photographs, and statistics about Olympic skiing.

Karen L. Kenney. *Girls Play to Win: Skiing & Snowboarding*. Chicago: Norwood House, 2010. Those interested in learning how to ski will be appreciate this book, which features tips on the sport as well as a history about women who have excelled in competitive skiing.

Bode Miller and Jack McEnany. *Bode: Go Fast, Be Good, Have Fun*. New York: Villard, 2005. The skiing careers of Lindsey Vonn and Bode Miller have had some parallels as both emerged into stardom around the same time. This book is about the life of Miller both on and off the slopes.

Picabo Street and Dana White. *Picabo: Nothing to Hide*. New York: McGraw Hill, 2001. Covers the life and career of Picabo Street, who was a great inspiration to Lindsey Vonn.

Periodicals

Lorenzo Benet. "Olympic Skier Lindsey Kildow Recalls Wedding Jitters." *People*, October 20, 2007.

Rachel Blount. "Lindsey Vonn: On Top of the World." *Minneapolis StarTribune*, December 25, 2008.

Shaun Dreisbach. "Lindsey Vonn, Mia Hamm & Lisa Leslie: The Game Changers." *Glamour*, November 1, 2010.

Tim Layden. "Ready to Rock." *Sports Illustrated*, February 18, 2010.

Mike Lopresti. "Golden Lindsey Vonn: 'This Is the Best Day of My Life.'" *USA Today*, February 17, 2010.

Megan Michelson. "An Interview with Lindsey Vonn." *Skiing*, January 2010.

Austin Murphy. "Smashing Success." *Sports Illustrated*, March 10, 2008.

Bill Pennington. "Lindsey Vonn at the Summit." *New York Times*, February 7, 2010.

Nathaniel Vinton. "Olympic Star Lindsey Vonn Trades Racing Uniform for Bikini in *Sports Illustrated* Swimsuit Issue." *New York Daily News*, February 9, 2010.

Internet Sources

Alan Abrahamson. "Lindsey Vonn: Designed to Win." NBC Olympics, January 11, 2010. http://i.nbcolympics.com/news-features/news/newsid=389228.html.

Charlotte Massey. "Meet U.S. Skier Lindsey Vonn." *Time for Kids*, February 24, 2010. www.timeforkids.com/TFK/kids/news/story/0,28277,1967833,00.html.

Videos

NBC Winter Olympics. *2010 Winter Olympics*. This DVD features highlights of the 2010 Winter Olympics, including the skiing performances of Lindsey Vonn.

Epix. *Lindsey Vonn: In The Moment*. March 2011. www.epixhd.com/lindsey-vonn-in-the-moment.

Websites

International Ski Federation (www.fis-ski.com/uk/disciplines/alpineskiing). This site offers information from the governing body of international skiing. It features statistics and biographies of the premier skiers in the world, as well as a rundown of all the competitions that have taken place over many years.

Lindsey Is Epic (www.lindseyisepic.com/#/home). This website is dedicated to the achievements and lifestyle of Lindsey Vonn both on and off the slopes. It includes race results and a short interview with the skier.

Maria Riesch: The Official Website of the Alpine Ski Runner (www.mariariesch.de/en/en-index.php). Learn all about Von's strongest international rival on this site, which features a short biography of Riesch, as well as videos and race results.

Nancy Davis Foundation for Multiple Sclerosis (http://erasems. org). Find out more about this crippling disease from this site. Vonn is one of many celebrities to join the fight to find a cure.

Team USA: Winter Athletes (www.teamusa.org/athletes/find). This website features biographies and various bits of information about all the current athletes participating on a wide variety of U.S. winter sports teams. Become familiar with those who will be participating in the 2014 Winter Olympics in Russia.

U.S. Ski Team: Lindsey Vonn (www.usskiteam.com/alpine/ athletes/athlete?athleteId=1001). Offers highlights of Vonn's career, photos, and the latest breaking news.

Picture Credits

Cover: © Erich Schlegel/Corbis
AP Images/Alessandro Trovati, 29, 81
AP Images/Craig Lassig, 15
AP Images/Diether Endlicher, 19
AP Images/Giovanni Auletta, 38, 82
AP Images/Janet Hostetter, 13
AP Images/Kevin Frayer, 42
AP Images/Luca Bruno, 54
AP Images/Luis M. Alvarez, 75
AP Images/Marco Trovati, 33
AP Images/Nathan Bilow, 21, 24, 63
AP Images/Pat Wellenbach, 65
AP Images/Stefano Dall'Ara, 44
AP Images/Tony Talbot, 37
Bobby Bank/WireImage/Getty Images, 72
Brian Bahr/Allsport/Getty Images, 27, 31

Clive Mason/Getty Images, 61
Doug Pensinger/Getty Images, 11
Fabrice Coffrini/AFP/Getty Images, 57
Frazer Harrison/Getty Images, 70
Guenter Schiffmann/Getty Images, 52
Jeffery Mayer/WireImage/Getty Images, 18
Josch/AFP/Getty Images, 56
Julian Finney/Getty Images, 9
Michal Cizek/AFP/Getty Images, 84
Monte Isom/Sportschrome/Getty Images, 49, 78
Oliver Morin/AFP/Getty Images, 51
© Paul Chinn/San Francisco Chronicle/Corbis, 66
© Ron Niebrugge/Alamy, 40

About the Author

Marty Gitlin is a freelance writer based in Cleveland, Ohio. He has written more than forty-five educational books. Gitlin has won more than forty-five awards during his twenty-five years as a writer, including first place for general excellence from the Associated Press. He lives with his wife and three children.

	DATE DUE		T